Into the Shadows
Radical Vigilantes in Khatami's Iran

Michael Rubin

Policy Papers no. 56

THE WASHINGTON INSTITUTE FOR NEAR EAST POLICY

© 2001 by the Washington Institute for Near East Policy

Published in 2001 in the United States of America by the Washington Institute for Near East Policy, 1828 L Street NW, Suite 1050, Washington, DC 20036.

Library of Congress Cataloging-in-Publication Data

Rubin, Michael, 1971-
    Into the shadows: radical vigilantes in Khatami's Iran / by Michael Rubin.
        p. cm. — (Policy papers ; 56)
    Includes bibliographical references.
    ISBN 0-944029-45-0
    1. Pressure groups—Iran—History—20th century. 2. Iran—Politics and government—20th century. 3. Political violence—Iran—History—20th century. I. Title. II. Policy papers (Washington Institute for Near East Policy) ; no. 56.

JQ1787.9.P7 R83 2000
322.4'2'0955–dc21

                         00-047722
                         CIP

Cover photo © Corbis.
Cover design by Monica Neal Hertzman.

The Author

Michael Rubin, a native of Philadelphia, is currently a visiting professor of Iranian history at the University of Sulaymani in northern Iraq and a 2000–2001 Fellow of the Carnegie Council on Ethics in International Affairs. He received his Ph.D. in history from Yale University in 1999; his dissertation, entitled "The Formation of Modern Iran, 1858–1909: Communications, Telegraph, and Society," won Yale's prestigious John Addison Porter prize for the top dissertation in any field. He simultaneously served as a Lecturer of History at Yale University and a Soref research fellow at the Washington Institute for Near East Policy in academic year 1999–2000. He has also published numerous scholarly and policy articles appearing in such journals as *Iranian Studies; Comparative Studies of South Asia, the Middle East, and Africa; Jerusalem Report;* and *Middle East Quarterly.*

Dr. Rubin has traveled extensively in the Middle East, spending more than six months in Iran, five months in Central Asia, fifteen months in the Arab world—including nine months in northern Iraq—and shorter periods of time in both the Taliban and United Front portions of Afghanistan. He has held numerous academic and policy fellowships and, as a student, was a State Department intern in Israel, Bahrain, and Tajikistan.

• • •

Table of Contents

Acknowledgments

This Policy Paper was made possible by the assistance and advice of many others. I am grateful to Dr. Patrick Clawson, director for research at The Washington Institute, Michael Eisenstadt, senior fellow at The Washington Institute, and Dr. Abbas Samii, regional specialist at Radio Free Europe/Radio Liberty in Prague, for their guidance on the topic. I also thank Robert Satloff, executive director of The Washington Institute, and the Samuel M. Soref and Helene K. Soref Foundation for supporting my research. Research assistant Michael Moskowitz and intern Marcus Oliver helped gather background material and proofread drafts. Few could ask for a better copy editor than Alicia Gansz; Cheryl Weissman also assisted with copyediting.

Finally, I am grateful to my many friends in Iran, who exhibited traditional Iranian hospitality while generously providing guidance on many sensitive issues. I hope that one day soon, reform in Iran will run deep enough for me to recognize them publicly.

Michael Rubin
Sulaymani
May 2001

Preface

A mong the many political systems in the Middle East, the regime in the Islamic Republic of Iran stands out as one of the most peculiar. There, the formal government—president, parliament, and other official governing components—is paralleled by more powerful revolutionary institutions, as analyzed in *Who Rules Iran?*, a Washington Institute monograph by Dr. Wilfried Buchta (copublished in 2000 with the Konrad Adenauer Foundation). Now, The Washington Institute sheds light on a third strand in Iranian politics, namely, the vigilante groups used by hardliners to intimidate reformers with raw violence unchecked by legal norms.

Iranian vigilante groups present more than an abstract problem. Since President Muhammad Khatami's 1997 election—and as the power struggle between the Islamic Republic's reformist and hardline camps has intensified—hardline vigilante groups have become increasingly active, bold, and violent, while seeming to operate with impunity. Indeed, Iranian hardliners often use political and social crises as an excuse to unleash vigilantes against reformers, and then demand firm state action ostensibly for the sake of maintaining stability and national security. By participating in this vicious cycle, vigilante groups reduce the prospects for substantive institutional reform through Iran's limited democratic processes.

In this richly detailed Policy Paper, historian Michael Rubin presents an incisive and comprehensive survey of the vigilante or "pressure" groups, along with an exploration of the deep roots these groups have in modern Iranian history. Drawing on both a wide array of Persian language sources and his own research conducted in Iran, Dr. Rubin, a 1999–

2000 Soref research fellow at the Institute, concludes that—despite the inevitability of political change suggested by demographic and economic realities in the Khatami era—the prospects for real reform in Iran within the existing system of rule are weakened by vigilante activism.

In addition to undercutting Iranian domestic reform, vigilante actions challenge U.S. efforts to achieve a gradual rapprochement with Tehran. The strategic use of vigilantes by the regime therefore also raises important policy issues for the U.S. government. The United States, Dr. Rubin argues, should not tolerate a shell game in which pressure groups—sponsored by those in power—are used to carry out hostile actions for which the government then conveniently denies responsibility. If the Iranian president cannot effectively suppress the vigilantes, then he may be too weak a figure to implement meaningful changes in foreign or domestic policy.

Understanding the threat these vigilante groups pose can only improve America's ability to formulate effective policy toward Iran. To advance that goal, The Washington Institute is proud to present this important research.

Michael Stein
Chairman

Fred S. Lafer
President

Executive Summary

Hardline vigilante groups, generally referred to as "pressure groups" (*guruh-i fishar*) in popular Iranian parlance, have long influenced Iranian politics and society during times of political tension. But particularly since President Muhammad Khatami's 1997 election—as the power struggle between the Islamic Republic's reformist and hardline camps has accelerated—vigilantes have become increasingly active, bold, and violent. Seeming to operate with impunity, their actions threaten both to undercut Iranian domestic reform and to challenge U.S. efforts toward a gradual rapprochement with Iran.

Iranian pressure groups cannot be considered a part of the "opposition" camp because, in reality, they act *on behalf of* various hardline factions within the government. Rather than attempt to overthrow the regime, pressure groups instead use violence, intimidation, and assassination as tools to affect government policy when they may not have the numerical strength or the power to do so through legal or legislative means.

Several vigilante groups are operating in the Islamic Republic today. The three most prominent are listed below:

- *Ansar-i Hizbullah* (Defenders of the Party of God) is best known for its involvement in the July 1999 storming of a Tehran University dormitory, an incident that sparked the worst rioting in the Islamic Republic in two decades.
- **The "Sa'id Imami Gang,"** composed of Intelligence Ministry operatives and named after the former deputy minister of intelligence, stands accused of murdering a number of Iranian intellectuals and dissidents during Khatami's administration.

- *Fida'iyan-i Islam* (Devotees of Islam) attacked a busload of visiting American businessmen in November 1998. They also appear to be linked to the Sa'id Imami Gang.

But hardline pressure groups are not a new phenomenon in Iran. They were also active during the period of tension that followed the 1979 Islamic Revolution, as vigilante actions contributed toward the shaping of policy on many issues in the nascent Islamic Republic. Three pressure groups stood out during this era:

- **Students Following the Line of the Imam,** as a loose-knit group of students, seized the American embassy in Tehran in 1980. The images of hostages held captive for 444 days is seared onto American consciousness, but the students also succeeded in bringing down a number of more moderate government officials and in pushing the committee drafting the new constitution of the Islamic Republic to compose a more hardline, less democratic document.

- *Hujjatiyyah* **(Charitable Society of the Mahdi)** was one of many hardline pressure groups with roots in pre-Revolutionary Iran. Although this group and its vision of collective clerical guardianship (as opposed to rule by one Supreme Leader) eventually lost out in an internal power struggle, it did succeed in transposing its anti-Baha'i ideology onto the policies of the new Islamic Republic, and it still issues calls for a more radical Islamic cultural revolution through the closely linked Islamic Coalition Association. Although currently banned, Hujjatiyyah appears to have spawned a more violent offshoot in the *Mahdaviyyat* (Disciples of the Mahdi).

- **The "Mehdi Hashemi Gang,"** a radical group that operated with official backing from 1979 until the mid-1980s, fell into disfavor with governing authorities who sought to direct Iranian foreign policy down a more pragmatic, less radical path. As a result, members of the group repeatedly undercut Iran's experiment in pragmatic moderation by sparking violence in the region generally as well as within Iran itself. The group also notoriously exposed the secret U.S.–Iranian negotiations that led to the Iran–Contra scandal.

Vigilantism has followed a similar pattern throughout modern Iranian history:

- *Vigilante groups are small,* usually numbering fewer than 100 core members and perhaps only a few thousand loose supporters, yet they have an impact on Iranian policy that is disproportionate to their size.
- *Vigilante groups have official patronage.* Although the pressure group is convenient to those in government who are interested in advancing certain goals outside of official channels and diplomatic commitments, the Iranian government has repeatedly failed to contain vigilantes once they begin deviating from the regime's desired policies. Indeed, pressure groups have a history of surviving government crackdowns and re-activating after years of dormancy.
- *Vigilante groups are operationally organized in cells based on informal networking.* They mobilize quickly through both telephone alert and intelligence given by high-ranking individuals within the Islamic Revolutionary Guard Corps (IRGC), the Ministry of Intelligence, and other security services.
- *The primary targets of vigilantes are those advocating reform in Iran.* Many pressure groups, however, also hold virulently anti-Western views.

Vigilantes attack and intimidate writers, intellectuals, and reformers according to two possible scenarios. In the first scenario, the pressure groups precipitate an attack, suffer no adverse consequences for that action, and thereby win a battle against reform. In the second scenario, vigilante actions spark a crisis—as with the July 1999 Tehran University dormitory attack—and effectively create an excuse for the traditionally

xiii

hardline IRGC, *Basij* volunteer forces, Law Enforcement Forces, and Intelligence Ministry to crack down on reform. Either way, the vigilante groups and their hardline supporters win, and the reformists lose. Until the reformists find a way to interrupt this dynamic, any gains for real reform within the framework of the Islamic Republic will remain tentative.

Indeed, vigilante groups pose serious challenges to Iranian reformers and to any future rapprochement between Iran and the West. Every political and social crisis in Iran sets back the clock and gives hardliners an excuse to roll back reform, ostensibly for the sake of preserving internal stability and national security. Although the overwhelming victory of reformist candidates in the 2000 *Majlis* (parliamentary) elections reinforced Khatami's mandate for reform, many Iranian hardliners still oppose change, for both ideological and personal–political reasons. Not surprisingly, few hardliners find it in their interest to renounce power voluntarily, realizing that they will not likely win at the ballot box without compromising on their more radical positions. Vigilante groups, however, create an alternative—a way for hardliners to forestall reform without having to take direct responsibility for the violent acts precipitated toward that end.

The demographic and economic realities of Iran may combine to make reform inevitable, but the activities of the vigilante groups create doubt as to whether Iranian politicians can bring about real institutional change through Iran's limited democratic processes before the power struggle turns violent; in this regard, pressure groups can be a means to gauge the real ability of Iran's formal governing structures to control the situation on the ground.

Ultimately, the considerable capacity of vigilantes to engage in street violence and assassinate prominent officials without penalty raises the possibility that hardline vigilante action may create the spark that will ignite a more violent phase of reform. Hardline sponsors of pressure groups—Ayatollah Ahmad Jannati, 'Ali Fallahian, and perhaps even Supreme Leader 'Ali Khamene'i himself—might for now find the vigilantes a convenient means by which to reap the benefits of pressure exerted toward certain political ends while avoiding responsibility for the violent face of that pressure. But by maintaining what are essentially "brownshirts," these hardliners risk losing control of the vigilantes or of dissident individuals within those groups. Simply put, domestic vigilantism threatens Iran's very stability while at the same time encouraging violence, xenophobia, radicalism, and autocracy.

U.S. and Western policymakers should take Iranian hardline vigilante groups into account when constructing a coherent policy on Iran. If, on the one hand, the Iranian president is truly in control, he will be in a position to prevent other officials from funding elements devoted to violence and intimidation. If, on the other hand, the president cannot effectively suppress vigilantism, then any commitments he makes in the context of U.S. Iranian rapprochement may be called into question, as he may be too weak a figure with which to deal on major issues. The fact that many of the currently active pressure groups appear to be funded and protected not by wealthy eccentrics but rather by officials like Guardian Council chairman Ayatollah Ahmad Jannati and employees of Supreme Leader 'Ali Khamene'i suggests that such violence cannot be dismissed as an aberration. Although Western policymakers would like to see the triumph of reform in Iran and an end to official behavior that has reinforced that country's isolation, it would be inappropriate to hold out false hope if the Iranian government will not, or cannot, rein in the hardline vigilantes.

The goal of any U.S.–Iranian rapprochement should be the reestablishment of diplomatic relations, increased trade, and cultural exchange. But if rapprochement is ultimately to benefit both sides, then the West must continue to judge Iran on its rhetoric and not just on its actions. In this regard, the United States should seek real change in Iran and should not tolerate a shell game in which hostile Iranian objectives are surreptitiously maneuvered into the shadows of vigilante activity. Indeed, as long as hardline Iranian pressure groups that are funded, equipped, and protected by high-level officials continue to operate—potentially resulting in an attack on American diplomats or visitors—a U.S.–Iranian rapprochement runs the risk of provoking a backlash that could compromise any warming of relations.

Note on Transliteration

There are many methods of transliterating the Persian and Arabic alphabets into English. All are artificial. For the sake of consistency, however, Persian and Arabic names and terms have been transliterated largely according to the Library of Congress/*International Journal of Middle East Studies* system. Exceptions are made to allow for the common spellings of some recognized names (like Ayatollah Ruhollah Khomeini).

Table: The Evolution of Hardline Iranian Pressure Groups

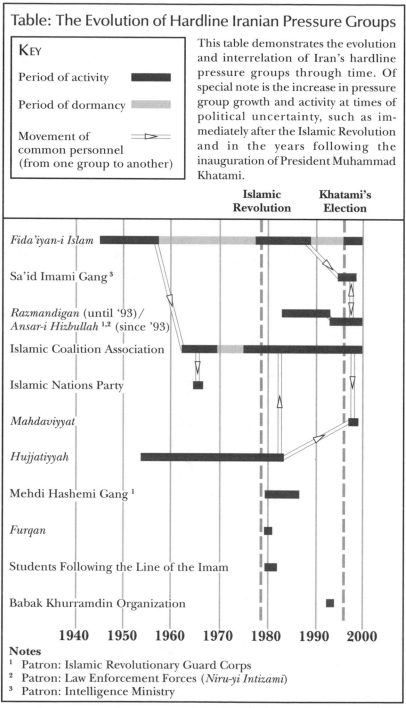

KEY

Period of activity

Period of dormancy

Movement of common personnel (from one group to another)

This table demonstrates the evolution and interrelation of Iran's hardline pressure groups through time. Of special note is the increase in pressure group growth and activity at times of political uncertainty, such as immediately after the Islamic Revolution and in the years following the inauguration of President Muhammad Khatami.

Islamic Revolution

Khatami's Election

Fida'iyan-i Islam

Sa'id Imami Gang [3]

Razmandigan (until '93) / Ansar-i Hizbullah [1,2] (since '93)

Islamic Coalition Association

Islamic Nations Party

Mahdaviyyat

Hujjatiyyah

Mehdi Hashemi Gang [1]

Furqan

Students Following the Line of the Imam

Babak Khurramdin Organization

1940   1950   1960   1970   1980   1990   2000

Notes
[1] Patron: Islamic Revolutionary Guard Corps
[2] Patron: Law Enforcement Forces (Niru-yi Intizami)
[3] Patron: Intelligence Ministry

© Michael Rubin, Washington, DC 2001

Chapter 1
The Historical Role of Pressure Groups in Iran

Vigilantes, commonly known as pressure groups (*guruh-i fishar*), have had a major impact on Iranian society over the course of the past century, affecting the political order and direction of Iran in a remarkable way, particularly during times of instability or ideological upheaval. Indeed, both before and since the 1979 Islamic Revolution, hardline politicians and prominent members of the clergy have employed the violence of pressure groups to achieve the political goals toward which they themselves cannot strive openly.

Although Iranian vigilantism dates from the turn of the twentieth century, it became a predominantly hardline phenomenon in the face of mid-century political instability and imperial pressure. Pressure groups, for example, helped direct street mobs during Prime Minister Muhammad Musaddiq's 1951 nationalization of the Iranian oil industry and the 1953 Central Intelligence Agency–supported coup that ended Musaddiq's administration. Vigilantes receded somewhat from prominence as the hardline regime gained greater control over society after the 1979 Islamic Revolution, but the groups have reemerged with a vengeance in recent years.

Iranian pressure groups possess unique characteristics that make them difficult to categorize in the context of Iranian politics. Despite enjoying support from government officials, they do not formally belong to the state structure. The groups cannot be construed as political parties, for they rely on violence, intimidation, and assassination rather than on legislative mandate to influence government policy. Nor are

1

they members of the revolutionary foundations (*bunyad*s) or the paramilitary *Basij* volunteer forces (quasi-governmental units that enforce public morality and other religious edicts). Yet, the vigilantes cannot simply be classified as "opposition" groups, because they effectively represent one faction within the Iranian government pitted against another. They neither seek to overthrow the existing regime—a goal of the Mujahidin-i Khalq Organization, for example (discussed later in the chapter)—nor claim to represent certain ethnic constituencies within the state, as do the Kurdistan Democratic Party of Iran or the South Azerbaijan National Liberation Committee. Sometimes pressure group members are simply called *hizbullahis*, literally, "members of the Party of God," although in popular parlance that label could also refer to recognized hardline members of the formal state apparatus or to the regime's unofficial hardline supporters.[1]

The vigilantes are often most effective when operating within small, tightly knit units, making them difficult to eliminate when they outlive their utility. Although the groups may sometimes become dormant, they seldom completely disappear. Even when seemingly immobilized, vigilantes tend to reemerge in times of political instability, such as during the early years of the Islamic Republic.

Hardliners and reformists alike acknowledge the existence of the vigilantes.[2] Indeed, the presence and impact of these groups is openly discussed in Iran—in official and popular circles, as well as in the media. Hasan Yusifi Ishkaviri, a writer for the reformist Iranian daily *'Asr-i Azadigan* (Age of the Free), once observed,

> If we look at the literature of some clerics, military men, leaders of parties, and especially some authorities of the Islamic Republic of Iran since the very first days of the victory of the revolution . . . we can clearly see that at least at certain junctures, pressure groups have been formed under different names . . . in order to confront political groups and rivals. On the other hand, there have always been official sources that have given political support to violent pressure groups in their statements, and also have con-

firmed them by ideologically and religiously theorizing their actions.[3]

Still, because pressure groups act according to a set of narrow principles and see themselves as accountable neither to the elected president nor to the Supreme Leader, politicians and religious figures have also tended to publicly distance themselves from the vigilantes.

An additional contributing factor to the rise and success of hardline vigilantism in Iran is the convoluted nature of the Iranian government.[4] Indeed, many different power centers and interests operate within the ruling structure, sometimes toward contradictory aims. Iranian society itself is riddled with various ideological schools of thought that represent profound differences in matters ranging from religious interpretation to economic theory. Within that convoluted structure, vigilante groups continue to serve as a means of bypassing institutional obstacles and advancing very specific anti-Western, anti-democratic, and anti-reformist goals.

Early History

Iran is one of only three countries to have experienced more than one major revolution during the twentieth century (the other two being Russia and China). Between 1905 and 1909, Iran underwent the Constitutional Revolution, wherein liberal nationalists and the clergy joined successfully to force the shah, Mozzafar al-Din, to accept both a constitution and a national consultative assembly (*Majlis-i shura-yi milli*).[5] During this revolution, secret societies known as *anjuman*s became a major force for change. Writing in 1910, Edward Granville Browne, a Cambridge University professor and well-known chronicler of the Constitutional Revolution, labeled "unofficial anjumans" as the "backbone" of the revolutionary popular movement.[6] Although the shah's government officially recognized some of those societies, it refused to acknowledge others. The latter openly agitated against the regime and continued to publish their own newspapers, distribute pamphlets, and arm their supporters.[7] Although the anjumans of the Constitutional Revolution were predominantly liberal nationalists as opposed to religiously based in their opposition to the shah's regime, later permutations of the societies maintained a distinctly religious nature, influenced perhaps by prominent religious figures who were funding such charitable groups and causes independently.

The societal upheaval that followed the Allied occupation of Iran during World War II fostered the development of several important pressure groups. When the war erupted, Iran remained officially neutral but appeared to be increasingly pro-German in the eyes of both Britain and the Soviet Union. Following Germany's June 1941 invasion of the Soviet Union, Britain and the Soviets demanded that Shah Riza expel German nationals from Iran so that the country would not become a launching pad for Nazi operations. When the shah refused, British and Soviet troops entered Iran on August 25, 1941, and forced him to abdicate in favor of his son, Muhammad Riza, who would continue the family's reign until the 1979 Islamic Revolution.

Shortly after Shah Riza's 1941 abdication, several Tehran University medical school students founded the *Anjuman-i Islami-yi Danishjuyan* (Islamic Students Association, or ISA), organized and run largely by figures who would later become influential in other capacities. Those figures included Mehdi Bazargan, the Islamic Republic's first provisional prime minister; Ayatollah Mahmud Talaqani, a leading cleric imprisoned by the shah just prior to the Islamic Revolution; and Yadullah Sahabi, a professor of geology at Tehran University.[8] The ISA published a platform calling for the Islamic reform of Iranian society, improvement in pan-Islamic relations, the proselytization of Islam, and religious purification of society. It challenged the "secularist propaganda" of Baha'i students and of the communist Tudeh Party. Soon, similar organizations emerged in such important provincial cities as Tabriz and Mashhad.[9]

Later, in a 1962 speech, Bazargan insisted that the anjumans were apolitical, but after his arrest by the shah's police and at his trial the following year, prosecutors argued that Bazargan had used the ISA as a cover for political agitation sponsored by the Iranian Freedom Movement, an opposition group founded in 1961 by Bazargan, Talaqani, and Sahabi. Although the two movements were separate entities, their membership rolls did, in fact, greatly overlap.[10] In his own defense, Bazargan insisted that religion had always been a locus of anti-government activities, and as such the various Islamic student associations should be considered quasi-official opposition groups.[11] In the end, the relationship between pressure groups and the Islamic hierarchy was allowed to remain murky and undefined during this period.

The Fida'iyan-i Islam: Formation to Revolution

In 1945, a twenty-two-year-old theological student named Sayyid Mujtaba Mirlawhi became angry at some controversial essays and books written by the prominent secular historian Ahmad Kasravi. Although best known today for his history of the Iranian Constitutional Revolution, Kasravi had argued in many of his works that traditional Shi'ism was responsible for many of Iranian society's ills.[12] Mirlawhi raised money from the clergy in Najaf, a Shi'i shrine city and educational center in Iraq (where Ayatollah Ruhollah Khomeini taught during the greater part of his exile), and he traveled from there to Tehran to debate Kasravi. After several encounters, Mirlawhi concluded that Kasravi was "evil." The former purchased a weapon and, in May 1945, seriously wounded the author. Mirlawhi was jailed but, when released on bail, he announced the formation of a radical religious group, which he called *Fida'iyan-i Islam* (Devotees of Islam).[13]

Upon founding the group, Mirlawhi invoked the uncompromising fundamentalism of the early Safavid dynasty, taking the alias Mujtaba Navvab-i Safavi (Navvab), or deputy of the Safavids (it was the Safavid dynasty, 1501–1722, that forcibly converted a largely Sunni Iran to Shi'ism). Navvab then dedicated the Fida'iyan-i Islam to fight "all forms of irreligion."[14]

Although, as a group, the Fida'iyan-i Islam remained largely distinct from a majority of the clergy, it maintained particularly close ties with Ayatollah Abul Qassim Kashani, whose views blurred the distinction between the clergy's spiritual and temporal powers.[15] During World War II, the occupying British and Soviet armies detained Kashani both because of his Nazi sympathies and because of the activities of his own pressure group, the *Mujahidin-i Islam* (Muslim Warriors).[16]

Although Kashani and his Mujahidin-i Islam never explicitly justified assassination to advance their aims, the Fida'iyan-i Islam exhibited no such restraint. In March 1946, just ten months after Navvab-i Safavi's assassination attempt on Kasravi, brothers and fellow Fida'iyan-i Islam members Husayn and 'Ali Muhammad Imami fatally gunned down Kasravi inside the corridors of the Ministry of Justice. Police quickly captured the Imami brothers as Navvab fled safely back to Najaf. He need not have done so; under considerable pressure from the clergy and the *bazaari*s (the traditionally conservative merchant class), a court acquitted the assassins.[17]

In July 1946, when Prime Minister Qavam as-Saltaneh ordered Kashani's arrest (on the grounds of Kashani's opposition to press censorship), the Fida'iyan-i Islam dedicated themselves to work for his release, which they won the following year. This episode bolstered the popular stature of both Kashani and Fida'iyan-i Islam.[18] In 1948, Kashani reinforced his populist reputation with a call for volunteers to fight against the newly declared State of Israel, a move for which he gained strong support in *Parcham-i Islam* (Flag of Islam), Fida'iyan-i Islam's newspaper. But the shah refused to permit 5,000 Fida'iyan-i Islam volunteers to go to Palestine to fight alongside Arab armies, highlighting the schism between the regime and Kashani's supporters.[19] Fida'iyan-i Islam subsequently participated in several violent clashes inside Iran, and it lobbied actively for parliamentary candidates supported by Kashani. Clearly, Kashani considered Fida'iyan-i Islam to be an effective pressure group at this point. Meanwhile, Kashani's Mujahidin-i Islam was still active in parliament, functioning as an extension of his religious faction (when Kashani later broke with the National Front in 1953, the Mujahidin-i Islam began to deteriorate).

In 1949, Fida'iyan-i Islam moved forward with its assassination campaign. During the shah's February visit to the
University of Tehran, the group made an unsuccessful attempt
on his life (when the police seized the shah's attacker, they
found in his pocket a *Parcham-i Islam* press card). In the wake
of this attempt, the Iranian government, already angered by
Kashani's call for nationalizing the British-dominated oil company in Iran (the Anglo–Iranian Oil Company), now deemed
Kashani's ties to the Fida'iyan-i Islam serious enough to war-
rant exiling him immediately to Iraq, from where he
proceeded to Beirut. Notwithstanding Kashani's exile, the
string of Fida'iyan-i Islam assassinations grew longer. In November 1949, Husayn Imami (who, with his brother, had
successfully eliminated Kasravi) gunned down Abdul Husayn
Hazhir, minister of court and a former prime minister, at the
Sipahsalar mosque in central Tehran.

The fact that one man, Husayn Imami, was at least partly
responsible for more than one Fida'iyan-i Islam attack indicates that the core of the group was small and without a large
number of operatives. Indeed, while Navvab claimed that the
group had 5,000 members and 100,000 sympathizers, the U.S.
embassy in Tehran estimated that Fida'iyan-i Islam membership was only in the hundreds at the time of the attacks.[20]
The group in fact was probably relying on the financial lar-
gesse of just a few wealthy sympathizers, whether maintained
by sympathy or extortion.[21] Even a relatively small donation
could generate an instant and significant impact in terms of
enabling Fida'iyan-i Islam activities.

In the meantime, authorities hanged Imami after an ex-
pedited trial; apparently, the shah had learned a lesson from
the leniency previously granted to Kasravi's murderers.[22] But
the deadly campaign of the Fida'iyan-i Islam was far from over.
In June 1950, Kashani, whose reputation had only been augmented by the spotlight of exile, returned to a delirious and
frenzied mob in Tehran. He continued working to pressure
the Iranian government to nationalize the Anglo–Iranian Oil
Company. But neither Kashani's religious leverage nor the
political pressure of his allies were enough to force Prime

Minister 'Ali Razmara (a general and former chief of staff) to effect a change in policy. On March 7, 1951, a twenty-six-year-old Fida'iyan-i Islam member named Khalil Tahmasbi shot and killed Razmara inside Tehran's Shah Mosque. Kashani lent his prestige to Tahmasbi's defense in court and won the assassin a "spectacular acquittal."[23] Whether or not Kashani ultimately gave the fatal order is not as significant as the fact that young devotees were still willing to engage in radical action on behalf of Kashani's guiding principles. That Kashani could maintain his distance from the assassination only augmented his ultimate effectiveness, thereby illustrating the way in which a respected political figure was able to benefit from the action of a vigilante group even in pre-Revolutionary Iran.

Razmara's assassination set the stage for the rise of National Front leader Muhammad Musaddiq. While the National Front and Kashani differed on some issues regarding the role of religion, they and their other allies in the Seventeenth *Majlis* (Parliament), 1952–1953 (Kashani, by this time, had won a seat in parliament), tended to share middle class roots and a distrust of the shah's increasingly royalist prerogative. Musaddiq did nationalize the Anglo–Iranian Oil Company in 1951, but his shaky alliance with Kashani did not last; Kashani's religious philosophy could simply find no room for the liberal political strains embraced by Musaddiq's National Front. Thereafter, the parliamentary alliances of Kashani's Mujahidin-i Islam stymied Musaddiq's attempts to acquire the full executive authority that would have bolstered his ability to negotiate effectively with the British government on the oil company issue. Musaddiq's failure to accrue greater powers from either the Majlis or the shah (who had refused Musaddiq his constitutional right to appoint the minister of war) ultimately led to the prime minister's resignation in 1952. Royalist Qavam as-Saltaneh replaced the popular premier, but Qavam himself resigned after a mere forty-eight hours, following violent demonstrations instigated by Kashani, who had called Qavam "the enemy of religion, freedom, and national independence."[24]

The very demonstrations that forced Qavam to resign his premiership returned Musaddiq to power with popular acclaim. But whereas Musaddiq and his National Front shared with Kashani an anti-imperial doctrine, they differed significantly on the role of religion. Having regained the premiership, Musaddiq proceeded to edge Kashani out of power, and by doing so, Musaddiq lost the support of the Mujahidin-i Islam, the Fida'iyan-i Islam, and the bazaaris.[25]

By August 1953, when Iranian royalist officers carried out a coup against Musaddiq and his most important government allies (with the support of the British government and the American Central Intelligence Agency), they were able to exploit the schisms between Musaddiq on the one hand and Kashani and his prominent clerical allies on the other. Shah Muhammad Riza, who had absented himself during the crisis, returned shortly thereafter and was welcomed by the latter.[26]

Once again firmly in control and unwilling to replicate his past mistakes, Muhammad Riza grew increasingly dictatorial. An alleged previous (1951) plot against Musaddiq by Fida'iyan-i Islam, as well as the group's assassination attempt against both a pro-Musaddiq member of parliament and newspaper publisher Husayn Fatemi further fueled the shah's anti-democratic crackdown.[27] But Fida'iyan-i Islam's abortive assassination attempt against Prime Minister Husayn 'Ala in November 1955 proved to be the last straw. With the acquiescence of the establishment clergy, the shah moved to crush the group,[28] and on January 18, 1956, the Iranian government executed Navvab and four of his top deputies.

The government also imprisoned Kashani in 1956, but the latter did not long remain behind bars. Ayatollah Husayn Tabataba'i Burujirdi, the highest-ranking Shi'i source of emulation at the time, interceded with the shah, who agreed to Kashani's release if the latter would completely disassociate himself from the Fida'iyan-i Islam and agree not to oppose the death sentences passed on the group's leadership.[29] Kashani so agreed, but, remarkably, neither Kashani's dissociation nor the execution of Fida'iyan-i Islam's top leaders spelled the end of the pressure group. Indeed, a core membership continued to carry out activities even after Kashani's quiet death in 1962, illustrating the difficulty faced by an Iranian government attempting to eradicate uncompromising hardline pressure groups—even when ultimately acting against their leadership.

Khomeini and the Islamic Coalition Association

In 1979, Ayatollah Ruhollah Khomeini became a household name in America, but his influence in Iran was much more extensive. Born, according to various sources, between 1899 and 1902, Khomeini received an early religious education in Arak and then in Qum's famous Madrasa-yi Fayziya, the most important seminary in Iran. In 1943, he published a book arguing for the creation of an Islamic government, but remained relatively quiet in his criticism of Shah Muhammad Riza's regime until the early 1960s.

One of the keys to Khomeini's rise to public prominence and power was the existence of both official and secret apparatuses inside his organization. In 1962, as Khomeini began his public campaign of protest against the shah's policies, he assembled followers into three different study circles that together would form the Islamic Coalition Association (ICA), sometimes also called the Coalition of Islamic Societies.[30] Students close to Khomeini oversaw the ICA, while each study circle nominated three members to join a central ICA leadership that would direct executive, financial, and propaganda committees. The association quickly expanded into other important provincial cities—where ten-member cells distributed Khomeini's statements, published leaflets, and encouraged general militancy against the shah[31]—and would prove crucial to sustaining Khomeini's program even after his arrest and exile.

In early 1963, the shah's government inaugurated the White Revolution, an ambitious privatization, land, and social reform program, which many conservatives among the religious clergy opposed. Khomeini himself would become a leader in the escalating the protests, not only against the White Revolution, but also against growing Western influence in Iran and the increasing autocracy of the shah's government. He preached openly against the shah's policies inside the Madrasa-yi Fayziya, and in March 1963, the shah's forces launched a bloody attack on the seminary, briefly detaining Khomeini himself. Following his release, however, Khomeini simply increased the vitriol of his attacks against the shah and his American benefactors.

Again, Khomeini became a target of the shah's security forces. He was ultimately detained on June 5, 1963, but was able to rely on the ICA and its cells to carry out his bidding. Within minutes, the ICA began spreading the word and mobilizing for protest.[32] As the shah's police rounded up Khomeini supporters, the ICA formed an armed wing composed largely of former Fida'iyan-i Islam members.[33] This armed wing drew up a long list of targets for assassination, including the shah himself and thirteen leading figures in his government. The group's first victim was Prime Minister Hassan 'Ali Mansur, whose murder led to the execution of four of the group's members and the arrest of twelve others, including 'Ali Akbar Hashemi Rafsanjani, Muhammad Beheshti, and Murtaza Mutahhari.

As Khomeini began his exile in 1964, the ICA continued to act to advance his personal ideology within the guidelines that he himself had established. On January 21, 1965, several members of the ICA, operating as part of another vigilante group known as the Islamic Nations Party (*Hizb-i Millal-i Islami*), gunned down Prime Minister Hasan 'Ali Mansur after he granted new contracts to foreign oil companies.[34] As with earlier Fida'iyan-i Islam attacks, the event sparked a crackdown that led to the arrest and execution of most of the ICA's political and military leadership. An ensuing investigation led to the discovery that many Islamic Nations Party members were former Fida'iyan-i Islam activists.[35] The ICA itself survived by claiming to redirect its attention to the nonpolitical and thus noncontroversial issue of education, forming several schools modeled upon the national curriculum but emphasizing religious education.[36] Although the ICA seemed to lie dormant for several years thereafter, it later claimed to have merely been preparing for armed struggle in the 1970s under the leadership of such personalities as Muhammad 'Ali Raja'i, future prime minister of the Islamic Republic; and Muhsin Rafiqdust, former Islamic Revolutionary Guard Corps (IRGC, or Revolutionary Guard) chief and later head of the Foundation for the Oppressed and Disabled (*Bunyad-i Janbazan va Mustaz'afan*)—a conglomerate indirectly linked to the financing of Iran's terror apparatus abroad.[37]

Beginning in 1968 and throughout the next decade, Khomeini maintained contact with his allies and the ICA through Ayatollah Murtaza Mutahhari, a long-time supporter of Kashani who was also linked to the Fida'iyan-i Islam. Mutahhari had fought unsuccessfully to prevent the expulsion of Fida'iyan-i Islam members during the government's previously discussed crackdown on the group.[38] Mutahhari long resided in Qum at the Madrasa-yi Fayziya (which also formerly functioned as the local headquarters of Fida'iyan-i Islam), and was particularly active there in the Militant Clergy Association (*Jami'a-yi Ruhaniyat-i Mubariz*), an organization founded in the aftermath of Khomeini's 1963 uprising. Like the ICA, the Militant Clergy Association continues to function inside the Islamic Republic to this day.[39]

In June 1975, mass demonstrations against the shah organized in part by the ICA took the regime by surprise and led to the deaths of several dozen people as well as the arrests of perhaps 300.[40] Afterward, the ICA continued to coordinate activities, such as facilitating the distribution of Khomeini's taped sermons and speeches, and by 1977 the association had more than eight branches in Tehran alone.[41] Throughout Khomeini's years of exile until Mutahhari's death on May 1, 1979, at the hands of *Furqan* (a pressure group discussed in Chapter 2), Mutahhari successfully enabled Khomeini to reach the masses. Moreover, he oversaw the groundwork laid by the ICA for a successful Islamic Revolution in 1979. More significantly, the success of Khomeini's ICA—which reached its peak of influence with the 1979 Islamic Revolution—demonstrated to other religious hardliners the importance of cultivating a pressure group as a support structure.

But the Revolution signaled the end of neither the ICA nor the Fida'iyan-i Islam; it merely ushered in a new chapter for both groups as they evolved to fill new roles in the Islamic Republic.

Hujjatiyyah: Shadow Group of the Past and Present

In 1953, a group of Islamic clergy led by Shaykh Mahmud Halabi (who was close to both Khomeini and Muhammad Musaddiq) formed a society called the *Anjuman-i Khayriyyeh-yi Hujjatiyyah-yi Mahdaviyyat* (Charitable Society of the Mahdi), known in political discourse simply as the *Hujjatiyyah*.[42] Based in the northeastern city of Mashhad, and with the support of Ayatollah Burujirdi (who had intervened to free Kashani after his imprisonment), the society established a loose network of cells throughout Iran to harass, campaign against, and persecute the Baha'i, a religious group representing less than 1 percent of Iran's population. Indeed, the Hujjatiyyah came to describe themselves as the *Anjuman-i Zidd-i Baha'iyat* (the Anti-Baha'i Society).[43] Baha'i are anathema to Iran's hardline clergy. They and their Babi predecessors have been persecuted in Iran since the religion was established approximately 150 years ago. Islam teaches that Muhammad was the last of the prophets and the *Qur'an* was the final revelation. Therefore, the Baha'i belief that the teachings of a nineteenth-century Persian writer named Baha'ullah (the "Bab") constitute a further revelation brings their faith into direct conflict with Islam.[44]

In 1955, Shah Muhammad Riza allowed Hujjatiyyah-supported anti-Baha'i sermons to be broadcast on state media, but the ensuing mob violence spurred international pressure that forced him to cease such overt tolerance of the group.[45] Throughout the remainder of the shah's rule, the Hujjatiyyah and its affiliated organizations continued to agitate against the Baha'i but otherwise stayed out of politics. When the shah cracked down on various religious organizations in 1963 (preceding Khomeini's exile), he allowed the Hujjatiyyah and its affiliate, *Anjuman-i Tablighat-i Islami* (Islamic Propaganda Society), to continue to function, finding Hujjatiyyah's fiercely anti-communist beliefs useful.[46]

The utilitarian approach of the shah in this case provides another example of official toleration for radical pressure groups even before the establishment of the Islamic Republic. Although he may have viewed communism as the greatest threat to Iranian society at the time, the shah's tolerance of the anti-communist Hujjatiyyah was shortsighted.[47] As subsequent events would illustrate (the Hujjatiyyah organized against him during the Islamic Revolution), pressure groups may be used as convenient tools of the regime for short periods, but their radicalism quickly becomes a burden to ruling authorities. Moreover, as has been illustrated by the examples in this chapter, once a pressure group establishes even a loose network, it becomes more difficult to eradicate—even after its leadership has been exiled or executed. For the radically Islamist Hujjatiyyah, the shah's opposition to communism and his turning of a blind eye toward the persecution of the Baha'i were not enough to deter the group's commitment to an uncompromising religious platform.

Violence on Demand: The Rebirth of the Fida'iyan-i Islam

Ayatollah Ruhollah Khomeini's June 5, 1963, uprising left its mark on Iranian history in many ways. Not only did this event trigger the formation of the ICA's armed wing; it also led directly to the creation of many other armed groups. One such organization was the *Mujahidin-i Khalq Organization* (MKO, or Holy Warriors of the People),[48] which became an important force in the 1979 effort to oust the shah, but nevertheless antagonized Khomeini and his followers in the group's opposition to clerical rule. In 1971, another group, the *Fida'iyan-i Khalq* (Devotees of the People), formed along the same relatively Marxist lines as the MKO, although the latter portrayed itself as the more Islamic of the two.[49]

The combined efforts of the MKO, the Fida'iyan-i Khalq, and remnants of the shah's regime posed a leftist and Marxist ideological challenge—as well as the military threat—to Khomeini and his followers in the 1970s. In the wake of this challenge, Fida'iyan-i Islam again became officially active, declaring its full support for Khomeini in 1978. Although some of its members had remained active in the ICA, the movement itself had entered a long period of dormancy following the shah's crackdown in the aftermath of the coup against Musaddiq. Now, the terrorist activities the group would carry out in the name of Islam became a convenient tool by which Khomenei's government could marginalize other militant challengers.[50]

In May 1979, after the Revolution had begun, Ayatollah Sadiq Khalkhali, a judge in the Revolutionary Islamic courts and a close associate of Khomeini, became Fida'iyan-i Islam's chairman, revealing in an interview that he had been a member of that organization since his student days.[51] Under Khalkhali's leadership, Fida'iyan-i Islam wasted no time in returning to its campaign of assassination. On December 7, 1979, when the Revolution had been secured, a hit man from the group gunned down the shah's nephew, Shahyar Mustafa Chafik, in Paris.[52]

As Khomeini consolidated power, Khalkhali became chairman of the Revolutionary Courts, providing a window into how the hardline pressure groups operate when they have official support and/or connections. At the Revolutionary Courts, Khalkhali quickly became known for his brutality, sending hundreds of former officials, dissidents, and Kurds to the firing squads. He was a strong proponent of these public-style executions, dismissing defense attorneys as a "Western absurdity."[53] In the American political consciousness, Khalkhali became enshrined for jabbing the bodies of American servicemen killed during the aborted 1980 hostage rescue attempt, even displaying one of the dead American's skulls during a televised appearance.[54] But his vengeful brutality and the bloodbath that resulted (including a mass slaughter of ethnic Kurds and executions of prisoners condemned in "kangaroo courts") isolated Khalkhali even within the radical new government of the Islamic Republic. On December 7, 1980, the Majlis forced him to resign, albeit over questions of corruption.[55]

Finally, with Khomeini's power consolidated and Khalkhali fallen from official grace, Fida'iyan-i Islam ceased its attacks against alleged opponents of the Islamic Republic—at least as the Republic had been enshrined under Khomeini's leadership—and the group once again retreated from the limelight. In 1981, the Majlis approved a law banning some political parties and placing jurisdiction over other groups in the hands of the Interior Ministry.[56] Under sanction of this new law, the government immediately targeted all parties opposing the regime. Within a few years, the pressure groups that existed primarily to combat groups questioning the policies of the Supreme Leader—that is, the Fida'iyan-i Islam, Mujahidin-i Islam, the Islamic Republican Party, and Islamic Coalition Association—all disbanded, at least temporarily.[57]

This development well illustrates the typical behavior of hardliners in government toward vigilante groups. When faced with even mild opposition, regime members activate the vigilantes for purposes of terrorizing and even silencing opponents. When control has been consolidated and centralized, the leadership encourages these groups to fade into remission. The ebb and flow of vigilantism, in this regard, seems linked directly to the will of the Supreme Leader and his tight circle of hardline cohorts.

Notes

1. Farhad Khosrokhavar and Olivier Roy, *Iran: Comment Sortir d'Une Révolution Religieuse* (Paris: Éditions du Seuil, 1999), p. 193.

2. Amir Muhibbian, "A Terrorist Solution to the Reforms?!" *Risalat*, January 2, 2000, p. 2, in FBIS (LD0402132100); "Rezaie: Foruhar Murdered by Pressure Groups Affiliated with Zionists," Islamic Republic News Agency (IRNA), November 23, 1998.

3. Hasan Yusifi Ishkaviri, "On Margin of Khordad Tribunal: Common Literature," *'Asr-i Azadigan* (October 31, 1999), p. 2, in FBIS (MS2012113599).

4. For a general overview of Iran's governing structures, see Wilfried Buchta, *Who Rules Iran? The Structure of Power in the Islamic Republic* (Washington, DC: The Washington Institute for Near East Policy and Konrad Adenauer Stiftung, 2000).

5. Seeking to shift the historical debate, Iranian authorities have attempted to create greater linkage between the two revolutions by artificially boosting the role of the religious clergy in the Constitutional Revolution at the expense of the liberal nationalists. See, for example, *Chikideh Malalat-i Nakhstin Siminar bayn al-Malali, Nahzat-i Mashrutiyat* (Tehran: Institute for Iranian Contemporary Historical Studies, 1999); *Tarikh-i Mu'asir-i Iran* (Iranian contemporary history) 3 (Summer 1999), p. 10. Earlier, Ayatollah Ruhollah Khomeini had criticized the Constitutional Revolution as "a conspiracy worked out by the imperialist government of Britain . . . to take the laws of Islam out of force and operation by introducing Western laws." See Ruhollah Khomeini, *Islam and Revolution: Writings and Declarations*, trans. Hamid Algar (London: Routledge & Kegan Paul International, 1981), p. 32.

6. Edward Granville Browne, *The Persian Revolution of 1905–1909*, ed. Abbas Amanat (Washington, DC: Mage Publishers, 1995), p. 245.

7. See, for example, the recently republished *Ruznameh-i Anjuman-i Tabriz* (Newspaper of the Anjuman of Tabriz) (Tehran: National Library of the Islamic Republic of Iran, 1995). For the anjumans' role in the initial struggle against Shah Muhammad 'Ali (reigned 1907–1909), see Browne, pp. 200–205.

8. Hamid Algar, "Anjoman (ii. Religious)," in *Encyclopaedia Iranica*, vol. 2 (London: Routledge & Kegan Paul International, 1985), pp. 80–82. For the later roles played by these figures, see Ervand Abrahamian, *Iran between Two Revolutions* (Princeton: Princeton University Press, 1982).

9. Algar, "Anjoman," p. 81.

10. Ibid.

11. See Hamid Dabashi, *Theology of Discontent* (New York: New York University Press, 1993), pp. 338–339. Dabashi relies heavily on Bazargan's writings in *Mudafi'at* (Bellville, Illinois: Nazhat-i Azadi Iran, 1964).

12. Farhad Kazemi, "Fanaticism, Politics, and Terror," in *From Nationalism to Revolutionary Islam*, ed. Said Arjomand (Hong Kong: Macmillan, 1984), p. 160. Kasravi's *Tarikh-i Mashruteh-i Iran* (A history of constitutionalism in Iran) continues to be cited in every major Persian and Western-language study of Iran's constitutional movement.

13. Kazemi, pp. 160–161.

14. Abrahamian, *Iran between Two Revolutions*, p. 258; Yann Richard, "Ayatollah Kashani: Precursor of the Islamic Republic?" in *Religion and Politics in Iran*, trans./ed. Nikki Keddie (New Haven: Yale University Press, 1983), p. 108.

15. Today, this blurring constitutes the theological underpinnings of Khomeinism. See Richard Cottam, *Nationalism in Iran* (Pittsburgh: University of Pittsburgh Press, 1979), p. 152.

16. For a brief discussion of Fida'iyan-i Islam's relations with the clergy as a whole, see Shahrough Akhavi, *Religion and Politics in Contemporary Iran: Clergy–State Relations in the Pahlavi Period* (Albany: State University of New York Press, 1980), pp. 66–67.

17. Kazemi, p. 161.

18. Ibid., p. 162.

19. Ibid.

20. Ibid., p. 168.

21. Ibid., p. 169.

22. Ibid., p. 163.

23. Richard, pp. 108–110; Akhavi, p. 69.

24. Richard, p. 111; Abrahamian, *Iran between Two Revolutions*, p. 271.

25. Kashani's failure to grant Navvab and Fida'iyan-i Islam more power during his brief alliance with Musaddiq's National Front led to the breakdown of Kashani's own relationship with the Fida'iyan-i Islam, a schism exacerbated by the 1951 arrest of the group's top leadership (Navvab was not released until February 1953). Kashani's break with the Fida'iyan-i Islam illustrates the danger faced by Iranian politicians maintaining a close relationship with hardline pressure groups, as the latter are seldom willing to compromise or adjust their will to majority opinion. See Kazemi, p. 165.

26. Abrahamian, *Iran between Two Revolutions*, p. 279.

27. Kazemi, p. 166.

28. Akhavi, p. 72.

29. Abrahamian, *Iran between Two Revolutions*, p. 421; Elie Kedourie, "The Iraqi Shi'is and Their Fate," in *Shi'ism, Resistance, and Revolution,* ed. Martin Kramer (Boulder, Colorado: Westview Press, 1987), p. 152.

30. Baqer Moin, *Khomeini: Life of the Ayatollah* (London: I.B. Tauris, 1999), p. 80. For a breakdown of these circles and their membership, see Masud Kuhistani Nijad, "Introducing the Islamic Mo'talefeh [Coalition] Association [An interview with Mr. Habibollah Asgar Owladi]," *Guzaresh*, no. 93, October 1998, online at www.netiran.com/Htdocs/Clippings/DPolitics/981022XXDP01.htm

31. Moin, p. 81.

32. Ibid., p. 110.

33. Ibid., p. 161.

34. Abrahamian, *Iran between Two Revolutions,* p. 440.

35. Kazemi, pp. 166–167.

36. Moin, p. 178.

37. Moin, p. 180; Michael Eisenstadt, *Iranian Military Power: Capabilities and Intentions* (Washington, DC: The Washington Institute for Near East Policy, 1996), p. 71.

38. Hamid Algar, introduction to *Fundamentals of Islamic Thought,* by Murtaza Mutahhari (trans. R. Campbell) (Berkeley: Mizan Press, 1985), pp. 17–18.

39. Moin, pp. 179–180.

40. Moin, p. 180.

41. Ibid., p. 181.

42. Said Amir Arjomand, *The Turban for the Crown: The Islamic Revolution in Iran* (New York: Oxford University Press, 1988), p. 157; Moin, p. 66.

43. Abbas Amanat, "The Historical Roots of the Babi–Baha'i Persecution in Iran" (paper presented at the annual meeting of the Middle East Studies Association, Washington, DC, November 21, 1999), p. 2. I am grateful to Abbas Amanat for providing his manuscript.

44. Moojan Momen, *An Introduction to Shi'i Islam* (New Haven: Yale University Press, 1985), pp. 231–232.

45. Moin, pp. 66–67.

46. Amanat, p. 2.

47. For indications of the shah's anti-communist views, see Muhammad Riza Pahlavi, *Mission for My Country* (London: McGraw Hill, 1960), pp. 106, 129, 315–316.

48. Although the MKO (sponsored largely by Iraq), has some supporters in the United States and many more in Europe, it is without significant popular support inside Iran and thus, as primarily an external group, falls beyond the focus of this study. For an excellent scholarly review of the organization, see Ervand Abrahamian, *The Iranian Mojahedin* (New Haven: Yale University Press, 1989).

49. David Menashri, *Iran: A Decade of War and Revolution* (New York: Holmes and Meier, 1990), p. 76.

50. Another *Mujahidin-i Islam* (Society of Muslim Warriors) also announced its formation from the vestiges of several older Islamist pressure groups around the time of the Islamic Revolution. That this

organization shared its name with Ayatollah Abul Qassim Kashani's former pressure group was not coincidental; Mujahidin-i Islam also declared its support for Khomeini, and promised to fight enemies of the Islamic Revolution "by all means." See Menashri., p. 77.

51. Kazemi, p. 167.

52. Menashri, p. 142.

53. Ervand Abrahamian, *Tortured Confessions: Prisons and Public Relations in Modern Iran* (Berkeley: University of California Press, 1999), p. 125.

54. John Burns, "Iran's Former Hanging Judge Now Sides with Reformers," *New York Times*, October 23, 1999, p. A1.

55. Menashri, p. 173.

56. Asgar Schirazi, *The Constitution of Iran: Politics and the State in the Islamic Republic*, trans. John O'Kane (London: I.B. Tauris, 1997), pp. 125–126.

57. Ibid., pp. 128–129. Muhammad Mehdi 'Abd-i Khuda'i, the general secretary of the Fida'iyan-i Islam, stood as a candidate for president in the 1985 election won by Khamene'i, though for unannounced reasons the Council of Guardians later rejected his candidacy. See Schirazi, p. 105.

Chapter 2
The Evolution of Pressure Groups under Khomeini and Khatami

U pon seizing power after his triumphant return to Iran, Ayatollah Ruhollah Khomeini declared April 1, 1979, to be "the first day of God's government."[1] But the creation of a modern Islamic theocracy was no mean feat. The Islamic Revolution faced a series of power struggles that threatened to erode an already loose anti-shah coalition. For instance, despite Khomeini's overwhelming popularity, no overriding consensus existed as to the philosophical or policy parameters that the new clerical state should follow. Accordingly, political jockeying was intense and competing pressure groups once again made themselves known. As various factions fought to impose their own respective visions upon the emerging Islamic Republic, new vigilante groups alongside old ones—and even one reincarnation—entered the fray.

Furqan: Striving to Cleanse the Revolution by Blood

On April 23, 1979, three men shot and killed General Muhammad Valiullah Gharani, the Islamic Republic's first army chief-of-staff, as he walked near his home in central Tehran. Gharani's murder was the first assassination of a major political or military figure in the nascent Republic.[2] A group calling itself *Furqan* (freely translated as Differentiators of Right and Wrong) claimed responsibility and also executed a number of other high-profile attacks designed to cleanse the Islamic Revolution of "reactionary clerics," rich merchants, "Marxist atheists," and liberal politicians.[3] On May 1, 1979, Furqan assailants gunned down Ayatollah Murtaza Mutahhari as he left a Tehran dinner party at the home of Yadullah

21

Sahabi, cofounder of the Iranian Freedom Movement (See Chapter 1).[4] Mutahhari was a key figure in the Islamic Coalition Association and was also a close associate of Ayatollah Mahmud Talaqani, another cofounder of the Iranian Freedom Movement and perhaps the most liberal of the Islamic Republic's clerical leaders.[5] Four days later, Furqan gunmen shot and severely wounded Ayatollah 'Ali Akbar Hashemi Rafsanjani, then just a top aide to Khomeini and a member of his Revolutionary Council *(Shura-yi Inqilab*, the government-in-transition during the Islamic Revolution).[6] Other attacks by the clandestine group followed, claiming the lives of the Friday prayer leader in Tabriz and of Hojjatolislam Muhammad Mufateh, a member of both the Revolutionary Council and the Assembly of Experts (*Majlis-i Khubragan*, a popularly elected clerical body that rules on religious and spiritual matters, including the election of the Supreme Leader *[Vali Faqih]*). Unwilling to rely on the legislative process to combat those opponents in government with whom it had philosophical disagreements, Furqan simply sought to kill them.

In this case, the response of the Iranian government proved effective. It executed Abdullah Gudarzi, a leading figure in the group, along with many of his colleagues, and Furqan quickly disappeared from the political scene after 1980. From that result, the Iranian government took the lesson that a severe response to vigilante action could effectively suppress certain pressure groups. Only recently, with a reinvigorated power struggle in Tehran, has the group reappeared in official parlance.[7]

Students Following the Line of the Imam and the Consolidation of Hardline Power

In October 1979, approximately 500 students from three Tehran universities, incensed that the U.S. government had granted permission of entry for the deposed shah, met to plan an operation against the American embassy in Tehran.[8] On November 4, 1979, young revolutionaries calling themselves Students Following the Line of the Imam (*Danishjuyan*

Piru-yi Khat-i Imam) seized the embassy, capturing seventy hostages—mostly American. The captors released eighteen hostages within the first month and held the remaining captives for 444 days. Although Khomeini kept his distance from the hostage takers, the captors had well-established ties to the pro-Khomeini senior clerics, most notably Hojjatolislam Muhammad Musavi Khu'iniha, Ayatollah Sadiq Khalkhali (the new leader of the Fida'iyan-i Islam), and Khomeini's son Ahmad.[9] Khu'iniha's arrival at the embassy as prayer leader for the students lent official legitimacy to the hostage-takers and prevented them from being denigrated in sermons and in the Iranian press as leftists or communists.[10]

The initially aloof Khomeini quickly seized upon the students' action in order to weaken his opponents and consolidate power.[11] Hoping to diminish the influence of the Islamic Left and the nonclerical members of the government, the students and their clerical backers leaked classified diplomatic cables and documents found in the embassy that suggested collaboration between various Iranian officials and the Americans. Among the targets in that campaign was Khomeini's chief opponent, Prime Minister Mehdi Bazargan, the first prime minister of the Islamic Republic and cofounder of the Iranian Freedom Movement. Accordingly, the students denounced Bazargan's deputy premier Amir Intizam, Information Minister Nasir Minachi, and Naval Commander Admiral Mahmud 'Alavi, all of whom Khomeini's security forces subsequently arrested on the basis of information provided by the leaked documents.[12]

Meanwhile, Bazargan actively sought to resolve the embassy crisis, but he found himself unable to break the impasse. Impotent in the face of the radicals, who were increasingly encouraged by Khomeini, and lambasted by the Iranian press for meeting with U.S. National Security Advisor Zbigniew Brzezinski in Algiers just prior to the embassy seizure, Bazargan resigned.[13]

But the impact of this Students Following the Line of the Imam action was greater than simply a high-level shake-up. The hostage drama in fact came as the constitutional con-

vention, elected in August 1979, was debating a draft constitution for the Islamic Republic. As Bahman Baktiari, a scholar
of Iranian politics, demonstrates, the embassy crisis had a last-
ing impact on the convention by inflaming opinion and
marginalizing moderates during a time when key provisions
were being debated. In one significant example, convention
deputies decided to change an article in the proposed constitution regulating the granting of economic concessions to
foreign concerns: now, instead of being dependent upon
Majlis approval, the concessions would be "absolutely prohibited."[14]

The hostage crisis may have also augmented the strength
of the Guardian Council *(Shura-yi Nigahban,* or Council of
Guardians), the constitutional body responsible for ruling on
the constitutionality and Islamic correctness of all laws passed
by the National Assembly) at the expense of the more democratic Majlis. Baktiari notes that prior to the embassy seizure,
an average of sixty-nine out of the total eighty-six members
of the popularly elected Assembly of Experts attended the
Assembly's sessions; after the embassy seizure, only fifty-two
attended on average.[15] Even the student radicals responsible
for the seizure have since acknowledged the deleterious impact that the hostage crisis ultimately had on the future of
Iranian democracy, as hardliners continued to utilize the
strength of the Guardian Council to limit the influence of
those deemed too reformist. On the eve of the twentieth anniversary of the embassy seizure, former captor Muhammad
Ibrahim Ashgarzadeh, now managing director of the Iranian
National Steel Company—himself recently attacked by vigilante students at Tehran University—admitted that the actions
taken by the Students Following the Line of the Imam in the
embassy seizure contributed to weakening the more democratic institutions of the Islamic Republic.[16]

Indeed, the radicalization caused by Students Following
the Line of the Imam during this episode formed a backdrop
against which the debate over the future role of governmental institutions would take place. Accordingly, the
hardline-dominated Guardian Council was invested with ex-

treme power to disqualify candidates deemed reformist, liberal, or too secular.

The Hujjatiyyah: Transition from Bigotry to Governance

Although never completely dormant, the Hujjatiyyah reemerged during the political tension of the early Khomeini years.[17] Khomeini initially embraced the group, perceiving that its anti-communist stance could act as a hedge against the rising prominence of leftists in the revolutionary movement.[18] The Hujjatiyyah quickly rose to distinction as the minority faction in the Majlis, while the dominant faction, the *Maktabis*, consisted primarily of students whom Khomeini led during his long exile in Iraq. The basis of the division between the Hujjatiyyah and the Maktabis was a dispute over who was eligible to succeed Khomeini after his death. While both subscribed to *vilayat-i faqih* (guardianship of the jurisprudent), the Maktabis argued that a single *marja'-i taqlid* (source of emulation) should succeed him, whereas the Hujjatiyyah favored a collective guardianship. As a result of this aspect of the dispute, the Maktabis often accused the Hujjatiyyah of being disloyal to the central idea of vilayat-i faqih. The Hujjatiyyah also favored greater practical separation between the clergy and government than did the majority Maktabis, although, true to their anti-Baha'i roots, the former sought a more radical Islamic cultural revolution.[19]

Ultimately, the Maktabis prevailed in the succession dispute, but the impact of the Hujjatiyyah was still significant. Although Khomeini and his followers held a majority in the Majlis and, more importantly, in the IRGC, the Hujjatiyyah retained its majority in the Islamic Republican Party (an umbrella organization of pro-Khomeini radical theocratic–Islamic groups) and in some sections of the Islamic Republic's Judiciary. A 1981 Mujahidin-i Khalq bombing of the Islamic Republican Party headquarters, however, resulted in deaths among the Hujjatiyyah's most prominent leadership—including President Muhammad 'Ali Raja'i—and the group subsequently began to lose its influence.[20] Even so, according to the Baha'i National Spiritual Assembly in London, the

Hujjatiyyah spearheaded the Islamic Republic's anti-Baha'i drive that, by 1983, had precipitated the execution of dozens and the imprisonment or disappearance of around 200 more.[21]

In August 1983, in the wake of the discussions taking place in the Assembly of Experts about succession, the hardline Iranian state media, having previously failed to acknowledge the Hujjatiyyah's existence, began an intense campaign against the group. Various articles in *Kayhan* and *Ittila'at*—both state-controlled, daily newspapers—condemned the Hujjatiyyah for what they called a lack of revolutionary fervor prior to 1979, and accused them of insufficient belief in the principle of clerical rule. Published interviews and editorials further accused the Hujjatiyyah of advocating monarchical Islam and favoring Shaykh Mahmud Halabi, the group's head, as Supreme Leader, rather than Khomeini.[22] After just two weeks, the public anti-Hujjatiyyah campaign ended when Halabi abruptly left Tehran for internal exile in Mashhad.

The Hujjatiyyah eventually dissolved into two groups after Halabi's departure: the ICA absorbed many members of Hujjatiyyah's more moderate wing, while some radical Hujjatiyyah members apparently formed a new and shadowy group called the *Mahdaviyyat* (Disciples of the Mahdi). Meanwhile, although the Hujjatiyyah itself faded from the political scene, it did not disappear altogether. The group occasionally resurfaced in political discourse in the late 1980s and 1990s, particularly during the intense power struggle surrounding reform-minded President Muhammad Khatami's 1997 election.[23]

The ICA under Khatami

The ICA, now counting many former Hujjatiyyah members among its ranks, continues to operate openly in the Majlis, along with other hardline factions like the pragmatic Servants of Reconstruction (*Kargazaran-i Sazandighi*), the radical Militant Clergy Association (*Jami'a-yi Ruhaniyat-i Mubariz*), and the more moderate Militant Clerics Association (*Majma'-yi Ruhaniyun-i Mubariz*), with whom it has intentionally worked in unison.[24] Closely affiliated with the religiously conservative Tehran bazaaris, the ICA has seen its own power diminish—at least formally—with the reformist victory in the 2000 Majlis elections.[25] Because of its links to other pressure groups, however, the association still enjoys a disproportionate capacity in the Majlis to act as an impediment to reform and diplomatic rapprochement with the West.

The two current leading figures of the ICA are Secretary General Habibullah Asgarawladi, a leader of one of the three original ICA constituent groups and a former minister of trade in both the Raja'i and Khamene'i cabinets; and Asgarawladi's deputy, Akbar Parvaresh. The ICA has been particularly active in its criticism of the United States and Israel, both of which, it claims, seek to create unrest in Iran. But the association is also highly critical of the Iranian reformist press, which it accuses of sowing discord.[26] Like many other pressure groups, the ICA controls its own newspaper, *Risalat*, which it uses as a mouthpiece.[27]

Asgarawladi himself is strongly associated with the use of violence for political purposes. In a March 1998 interview, for example, he expressed his continued sympathy for the religiously motivated violence of other vigilante groups. He also voiced no regret for the ICA's 1965 assassination of Prime Minister Hasan Ali Mansur; Asgarawladi's only concern was that armed groups like the Mujahidin-i Khalq Organization—which, unlike the vigilante groups, seeks to violently overthrow the entire government—had filled part of the vacuum left by the shah's subsequent execution of leading ICA figures.[28] Following the July 1999 rioting sparked by the combined attack of the Law Enforcement Forces (*Niru-yi Intizami*) and *Ansar-i Hizbullah* on a student dormitory (See Chapter 3), Asgarawladi sought to deflect blame from the hardliners onto those "who ordered the students to take to the streets and stage illegal demonstrations at midnight before the incident at the university dormitory occurred."[29] Other prominent ICA members, among them 'Asadullah Ladjvardi (former head of the Evin prison, assassinated by the Mujahidin-i Khalq in 1998) and Muhsin Rafiq-Dust (former chief of the IRGC and, until recently, head of the powerful, hardline Foundation for the Oppressed and Disabled), share similar hardline views.[30]

Mahdaviyyat: Hujjatiyyah's Most Recent Successor

A series of murders in 1998 and 1999 targeting intellectuals and dissidents (See Chapter 4) did much to aggravate the tension surrounding the surprising 1997 victory of Muhammad Khatami. When, on January 5, 1999, unidentified men attempted to assassinate Tehran's Judiciary chief, Hojjatolislam 'Ali Razini, who is head of the Special Clerical Court and a leading ally of current Supreme Leader 'Ali Khamene'i, the reformist daily *Salam* and the hardline *Jahan-i Islam* both blamed agents of the Hujjatiyyah for the attack.[31]

Although tainted by an undue credence lent to conspiracy theories, the *Salam* article went on to explain that the perpetrators had drawn up a list of figures targeted for assassination in the messianic belief that the Hidden Imam would not return while those responsible for establishing the Islamic Republic remained in power.[32] According to *Salam*, not only were the would-be assassins members of the underground Hujjatiyyah society, but they were also affiliated with the IRGC and the paramilitary Basij volunteer forces, a charge disputed by the hardline *Kayhan* daily.[33]

Before long, however, murky links between the vigilantes and the IRGC emerged. In April 1999, Brigadier General Muhammad 'Ali Jafari, commander of the IRGC ground forces, announced the arrest of an assailant named "Milani" (the IRGC announcement that followed Milani's arrest, as well as subsequent press reports, refer to him only by his first name) in the attempted assassination of Razini; Milani was a cleric and grandson of Ayatollah Sayyid Muhammad Hadi Milani, an important religious leader and early contemporary of Khomeini.[34] Jafari told the state-controlled Islamic Republic News Agency (IRNA) that Milani headed a new organization called the Mahdaviyyat—distinct from Hujjatiyyah and composed of a cabal of thirty religious extremists, including an Iran–Iraq War veteran explosives expert and another former IRGC member. Jafari also accused the Mahdaviyyat of stealing approximately 100 guns from Basij bases in Tehran's mosques. Although such an accusation may

have been an attempt by Jafari to stop Iranian press speculation that the IRGC was itself involved in the assassination
attempt, Jafari may also have sought to make a distinction
between the Mahdaviyyat and ICA members in the Majlis and
Guardian Council, so as to stop speculation that hardline
politicians might be directly involved.[35]

Mass arrests of Mahdaviyyat members followed Milani's
confessions (reported second-hand by Jafari), but the group's
activities persisted. On November 25, 1999, a statement by
the Intelligence Ministry (*Vizirat-i Ittila'at va Amniyat-i Kishvar,*
literally, Ministry of Information and Security) announced
the arrests of fourteen Mahdaviyyat members whom the ministry alleged had planned to assassinate President Khatami,
former President Hashemi Rafsanjani, and former Judiciary
Chief Ayatollah Muhammad Yazdi. The Intelligence Ministry
accused Mahdaviyyat members of stealing fifty-three weapons and a "considerable amount" of ammunition from various
Basij bases, establishing bomb-making workshops, and attempting to sow discord by attacking prominent Sunni
clergy.[36] For these crimes, the ministry specifically blamed "a
'deviate cleric,' who had penal records at the Special Clerical
Court and completed theological studies abroad, resided in
Mashhad since 1976 and [initiated] considerable activities
by launching an intellectual current" as well as a clandestine
armed group.[37] This biography would seem to describe Shaykh
Mahmud Halabi, leader of the Hujjatiyyah.[38] Whether or not
Halabi had anything to do with these incidents, by insinuat-
ing that he had, Iranian authorities acknowledged the power
of pressure groups to carry out such actions. Conversely, if
some Iranian authorities were indeed behind the attacks, it
would illustrate the tendency of these leaders to blame pressure groups in order to excuse their own involvement.

In particular, the Mahdaviyyat's strategy of sowing discord
among the Sunnis may work to the advantage of Iran's
hardliners by providing an excuse for a national security crackdown. Although Sunnis make up just 10 percent of Iran's
population, sectarian differences and the demographically
shifting presence of large numbers of predominantly Sunni

Afghan refugees make sectarian issues extraordinarily sensitive (recent Iranian government publications have even omitted the presentation of a Shi'i/Sunni population breakdown).[39] Iran's governing hierarchy is overwhelmingly Shi'i, and many of the Sunnis are ethnic minorities—Kurds, Baluchis, or Azeris. Accordingly, targeting of Sunnis can potentially threaten the legitimacy of Iran as a multi-ethnic state. In 1994, for instance, sectarian violence erupted (mostly in Baluchistan [a strategic area bordering the Pakistani province of the same name], outside the eye of the media) after the Iranian government destroyed a Sunni mosque in Mashhad (the country's second largest city).[40] The violence was severe enough for the government to call on the IRGC to suppress the demonstrators. There were retaliatory bombings in Mashhad, and a presumably Sunni assailant attempted to assassinate President Rafsanjani.[41] Ongoing concern about the possibility of attacks against Sunni clergy could create enough instability in Tabriz (the major city of northern Iran), Mashhad, and Baluchistan for hardliners to justify both a crackdown and a rollback of reforms.

More broadly, the existence of the Mahdaviyyat raises many interesting issues concerning relations between the Islamic Republic and the vigilante groups:

- The thefts of weapons from Basij bases may indicate that the Basij—the official hardline paramilitary group of the regime—has become a breeding ground for vigilantism. This is actually consistent with evidence linking other pressure groups to the IRGC, suggesting that this hardline military force also breeds "illegal" vigilantism.

- Acknowledgment by the Intelligence Ministry of Mahdaviyyat's existence would seem to set the stage for future attacks purported by the group against the Sunni minority. When an attack does occur, the Iranian government can simply deflect blame onto this shadowy group, even if the regime itself is ultimately responsible.

- If, however, the Mahdaviyyat is truly an independent group without ties to the government, then its very existence represents the danger to regimes of flirting with pressure group sponsorship. At one point, Khomeini found Hujjatiyyah to be convenient, but now, two decades later, the Islamic Republic has yet to find itself able to control Hujjatiyyah's renegade offspring and other similar vigilante groups that it once used as proxies. Evidence would seem to indicate that although some of its former members were absorbed by the ICA, and although the latter remains a perfectly legal faction within the Majlis, the seemingly defanged ICA–Hujjatiyyah may yet be maintaining a covert, hard-core faction intent on furthering its aims outside governmental constraints.

The "Mehdi Hashemi Gang"

The Hujjatiyyah was unique in that its dissolution was remarkably nonviolent. Its adherents simply joined the ICA or the Mahdaviyyat. Iran's experience with the so-called "Mehdi Hashemi Gang," however, reinforces the idea that using pressure groups might be convenient in the short term for specific—albeit unsavory—regime policy objectives, but in the long term, governmental authorities can quickly lose control over the radicals they have armed.

Born in Iran in 1941, Mehdi Hashemi received guerrilla training in Lebanon.[42] He gained early fame when, in April 1976, the shah's regime accused him, along with three colleagues, of abducting and strangling Ayatollah Abulhasan Shamsabadi, a prominent pro-shah religious leader.[43] Sentenced to death after a three-day trial, Hashemi became a *cause célèbre* among religious activists despite his televised confession. Iranian students in Paris and religious activists inside Iran rallied for his release.[44]

With the success of the Islamic Revolution, Hashemi was well positioned for assuming power. His brother, Hadi Hashemi, married the daughter of Ayatollah Husayn 'Ali Montazeri, a figure of central importance in Iran. Montazeri served as Khomeini's deputy and designated successor until his removal shortly before Khomeini's death, as discussed below. Under house arrest during much of the past decade, Montazeri is perhaps the highest-ranking religious opponent to the concept of *vilayat-i faqih*, or guardianship of the juris-prudent. As such, he presents an even more ominous challenge to the regime by attacking not just the system itself but its theological underpinnings. Although an initially strong supporter of vilayat-i faqih, he slowly rethought his stance when he saw problems in the implementation stages of the concept. The fact that he spoke up, and thus sacrificed his chances to become Khomeini's successor, further augmented Montazeri's image among the quietist religious opposition.

For his part, Mehdi Hashemi was able to use his close association with Montazeri to ascend within the Iranian power structure. He headed the now-defunct Office of Liberation Movements, a formal arm of the IRGC designed to coordi-nate export of the revolution until, in 1982, the government began to treat this office as an entirely separate entity (it con-tinued to function out of Montazeri's headquarters in Qum).[45] No longer officially part of the government, Hashemi's Of-fice of Liberation Movements continued to actively assist Hizbullah in Lebanon and the Mujahidin in Afghanistan with with covert regime support.[46] By using Hashemi, the Iranian government was able to advance its more violent interests abroad while avoiding official linkage.

But Hashemi's radicalism and strong advocacy of violent religious extremism eventually clashed with the government's changing priorities. In 1986, as casualties were mounting in the war with Iraq, little evidence existed to suggest that the conflict could be ended militarily. Rafsanjani and Foreign Minister 'Ali Akbar Velayati were particularly concerned that states on the Gulf Cooperation Council were continuing to finance the Iraqi war machine, and they consequently under-took a diplomatic initiative to repair Iran's relations with the Arab world.[47] Meanwhile, in August 1986, Hashemi allegedly sent Iranian operatives disguised as pilgrims to the *Hajj* (the official Muslim pilgrimage to Mecca) in Saudi Arabia, where Saudi authorities were said to have arrested more than 100

Iranians carrying arms and explosives. Iranian prime minister Mir Husayn Musavi vigorously protested this incident to the Saudi government, as the Iranian official newspaper *Kayhan* reported that many of the pilgrims were arrested for carrying no more than political tracts and pictures of Khomeini.[48] Despite Musavi's attempt at face saving, the incident reportedly embarrassed Velayati and Rafsanjani and undermined the credibility of their diplomatic initiative toward the Arab Gulf regimes.[49]

Not long afterward, Hashemi further infuriated Rafsanjani by allegedly ordering the kidnapping of Mahmud Ayat, the Syrian chargé d'affaires in Tehran. Gunmen pulled Ayat from his car in Tehran on October 3, 1986, but released him unharmed later that evening. Although Hashemi blamed the Intelligence Ministry for the operation, he may have had his own ideological motivation: notwithstanding Syria's role as Iran's chief Arab backer in the war with Iraq, the Syrian and Iranian leaderships held conflicting views about whether Lebanon should be subservient to a Greater Syria or rather should become a theocratic state modeled after Iran.[50] If Hashemi was indeed behind these two incidents, then the independent actions of his pressure group clearly ran counter to the shifting priorities of the ruling regime, which sought to take a more pragmatic view toward alliances—even if that pragmatism meant contravening ideological stances.

Indeed, the Islamic Republic is consistently known to adopt pragmatic foreign policy positions. As a well-known recent example, in consideration of Russian assistance—official or otherwise—for Iranian weapons programs, Iran chose to mute its criticism of Russian actions in Muslim Chechnya in the late 1990s (Iran was chair of the Organization of the Islamic Conference at the time and was expected to protest these actions vehemently). Mehdi Hashemi, however, was consistently unwilling to compromise his radical principles for the sake of his government's often more nuanced position. Rather, he was fully prepared to take advantage of an opportune moment to undermine those he considered too moderate. For Supreme Leader Khomeini and President

Rafsanjani, Hashemi's activities might have been convenient during the early years of the Revolution, but as the Iran–Iraq War dragged into its sixth year of stalemate, he was quickly becoming a liability.

The Iran–Contra Affair

Perhaps the most extraordinary example of the conflict between pragmatism and ideology in Iranian foreign policymaking took place in the 1980s in what became known in the United States as the Iran–Contra Affair. This infamous episode crippled the Reagan administration politically for several years. In Iran, it led to the downfall of the Mehdi Hashemi Gang.

The storyline of the Iran–Contra Affair is complex. In 1983, in an attempt to win the release of American hostages in Lebanon and circumvent congressional restrictions on funding for the Nicaraguan resistance (the Contras), high-ranking officials of the Reagan administration began to sell arms and spare parts for weapons to Iran for use in its war against Iraq. Proceeds from those sales were then rechanneled to support the Contras in their fight against the Sandinista government.[51] As became apparent, prominent Iranian politicians like then-Majlis Speaker Hashemi Rafsanjani and Chairman of the Majlis Foreign Affairs Committee Hadi Najafabadi, were involved in the secret contacts that facilitated the exchange. Clearly, in this case, Iran's military need for spare parts trumped the regime's ideological antipathy toward Israel and the United States.[52]

A week after U.S. national security advisor Robert McFarlane departed from Iran in the context of his March 1986 visit, pamphlets traced to Hashemi that reported "the visit of an American official" were tacked onto bulletin boards at the University of Tehran.[53] Several months later, on November 3, 1986, the day before the anniversary of both Khomeini's 1963 arrest and the 1980 U.S. embassy seizure, *Ash Shiraa*, a pro-Syrian Lebanese news magazine, broke news of the secret contacts between American and Iranian officials.[54] Hassan Sabra, the magazine's editor, later revealed that his sources were representatives of Montazeri wishing to embarrass factions in the Iranian government that he saw as too willing to compromise on revolutionary ideals.[55] Subsequent reports in the Iranian media, however, indicated that Hashemi himself may have been the source, even though he was already in jail by the time *Ash Shiraa* broke the initial story.[56] Regardless, on November 4 an embarrassed Rafsanjani confirmed the account to the world press.

Suspecting that the Mehdi Hashemi Gang was indeed responsible for the exposé, Rafsanjani took action.[57] On October 12, 1986, the Iranian government arrested Hashemi and his followers, including Montazeri's son-in-law Hadi Hashemi. Montazeri rushed from his home in Najafabad (outside Isfahan) to Tehran to intercede with Khomeini, but to no avail.[58] (The event should not have surprised Montazeri, for Khomeini had warned him more than a week before the arrest.[59]) Khomeini requested that Montazeri keep quiet, but the latter nevertheless launched a private, impassioned, but ultimately unsuccessful defense of his son-in-law, praising Hashemi and criticizing Intelligence Minister Muhammad Rayshahri and Revolutionary Guard commander Muhsin Riza'i.[60]

On October 27, Tehran radio alluded to "certain arrests" that had taken place, including those of Mehdi Hashemi and some of his allies. The report, based on a letter by Rayshahri, indicated that those detained were charged with "murders committed both before and after the revolution, kidnapping, illegal possession of arms, forgeries, and attempts to cause divisions in the country."[61] Rayshahri later added charges of collaboration with the SAVAK (*Saziman-i Aminiyyat va Ittila'at-i Kishvar*, the shah's secret police), and revived the charge of Ayatollah Shamsabadi's murder.[62] In the mind of that portion of the Iranian public most unquestioning in its loyalty to the Islamic government, Mehdi Hashemi—almost overnight—went from being a hero of the Islamic Revolution to a dangerous counterrevolutionary.

On December 14, 1986, IRNA recounted Rayshahri's allegations at length. For his part, Rayshahri claimed that his investigation was initiated at the behest of Khomeini and was already two years in the making. He described Hashemi's followers as a vigilante group, reporting that "the aim of Mehdi Hashemi's group was to contaminate the seminaries, the clergy and the system with their deviationist ideologies." Rayshahri accused the "Mehdi Hashemi group" of circulating documents impugning the reputation of an unnamed Majlis deputy. Further investigation, Rayshahri alleged, revealed that Hashemi had been a SAVAK informant spying not only on Muhammad Montazeri (Ayatollah Montazeri's son, killed in the June 1981 bombing of the Islamic Republican Party headquarters) but also on the other suspects in the original Shamsabadi murder. Rayshahri went on to insist that his agents were able to identify a house that they linked to Hashemi and to several illegal activities. Perhaps shedding some light on the blurred distinction between politics and justice in Iran, Rayshahri continued, "I felt the issue was political and that the Information [Intelligence] Ministry might be smeared. I contacted the Imam's [Khomeini's] office. He commanded with decisiveness that the matter should be pursued." A search of the house allegedly revealed a wealth of contraband, from carcinogenic powders and cyanide to explosives hidden in fountain pens and remote-control model airplanes.[63]

Subsequent interrogations resulted in the arrests of forty alleged Mehdi Hashemi Gang members, some of whom had capital murder charges levied against them. At dawn on September 28, 1987, a firing squad at Tehran's infamous Evin prison executed Mehdi Hashemi, just six weeks after his conviction. In the following weeks, several alleged accomplices met the same fate. Hashemi may have been officially punished as "[one] corrupt on earth who wages war on God," but in reality this vigilante's crime was to have challenged Rafsanjani—and lost.[64]

Hashemi's death did not end the bogey that his pressure group represented to the Islamic Republic, however. The impact of this power struggle actually extended beyond Hashemi to Montazeri himself. Montazeri was allegedly infuriated by Hashemi's fate, and he blamed Rafsanjani personally. According to Baktiari, Montazeri thereafter antagonized Khomeini by supporting "every possible opponent of Rafsanjani," from radicals in the Majlis to the Iranian Freedom Movement (considered so liberal that the Council of Guardians has disqualified every candidate the movement has fielded for parliamentary or presidential elections since 1984).[65] Sparked by the Mehdi Hashemi affair, the schism between Montazeri and Khomeini grew and, on March 27, 1989, Montazeri finally resigned.[66] Khomeini passed away shortly thereafter, on June 3, and the reins of the Supreme Leadership passed to hardliner 'Ali Khamene'i. Much later, Rayshahri would call Khomeini's decision to dismiss Montazeri "a shining point in the life of the late Imam."[67]

As late as November 1997, Montazeri publicly criticized the extent of power that Khomeini's successor, Supreme Leader Khamene'i, enjoyed and called for Muhammad Khatami, the newly elected president, to have more day-to-day control over the affairs of government. Vigilantes, perhaps members of Ansar-i Hizbullah, responded to that open criticism by attacking Montazeri's home and office in Qum, forcing him to flee under police protection. In February 1998, Khamene'i attempted to exert further control over Montazeri: an Iranian court froze his bank accounts, while the government prohibited him from receiving any visitors as he remained under virtual house arrest.[68] Even today, Montazeri is virtually cut off by a government cordon. Montazeri continues to enjoy wide sympathy among the Iranian populace, however, which views him as having sacrificed personally to criticize the excesses of the regime. As Khamene'i's grip on Montazeri tightened, pro-Montazeri protests erupted in March and April 1998. Khamene'i responded by issuing a stern warning to the protestors and also called for a counterprotest.[69] He ordered the arrest of at least fifteen people and sacked several officials deemed too sympathetic to Montazeri. Explaining the disturbances to a Western correspondent, an IRGC official reported that the "gang of Mehdi Hashemi [was] at the root of the trouble."[70]

On January 10, 1999, Shiraz Friday prayer leader Ayatollah Mohi'eddin Ha'eri-Shirazi accused those responsible for the 1998 dissident murders (See Chapter 4) of being Mehdi Hashemi Gang members, even though these murders were a crime the Intelligence Ministry later admitted to perpetrating.[71] In an August 1999 interview with the now-banned reformist newspaper *Neshat*, Majlis deputy Muhammad Javid Larijani referred to the Mehdi Hashemi Gang as a mafia-like group that exploited Montazeri's name, arguing that Montazeri's followers continued to give legitimacy to stances that undermined hardliners within the Islamic Republic.[72] Iranian society is anything but naive, however, and many see through such transparent hardline attempts to tarnish opponents with the "Mehdi Hashemi Gang" label. Ayatollah Jalal Taheri of Isfahan told *Arya* on January 12, 1999, that "whomever [Iranian government officials] want to remove from the scene, they say he's part of Mehdi Hashemi's gang."[73]

Notes

1. Ruhollah Khomeini, *Islam and Revolution: Writings and Declarations*, trans. Hamid Algar (London: Routledge & Kegan Paul International, 1981), p. 265.

2. Nicolas Cumming-Bruce, "Gunmen Kill Top General in Tehran," *Washington Post*, April 24, 1979, p. A1.

3. Ervand Abrahamian, *The Iranian Mojahedin* (New Haven: Yale University Press, 1989), p. 52.

4. William Branigan, "Shi'ite Leader, Tied to Iran's Rulers, Slain," *Washington Post*, May 2, 1979, p. A1.

5. Hamid Algar, introduction to *Fundamentals of Islamic Thought*, by Murtaza Mutahhari (trans. R. Campbell) (Berkeley: Mizan Press, 1985), p. 19.

6. William Branigan, "Ayatollah, Aide of Khomeini, Shot in Iran," *Washington Post*, May 26, 1979, p. A25.

7. In June 1999, the official government daily *Iran* quoted Kirman province's deputy governor as blaming a group similar to Furqan for kidnapping three Italian tourists. In this case, which involved Baluchi drug smugglers, the government invented a conspiracy involving the group to deflect attention away from what was actually a law-and-or-

der problem that could have embarrassed the regime. See Abbas Samii, "Italians Free but Questions Linger," Radio Free Europe/Radio Liberty (RFE/RL) *Iran Report* 2, no. 26, June 28, 1999; interviews by author in Kirman, August 10, 1999.

8. David Menashri, *Iran: A Decade of War and Revolution* (New York: Holmes and Meier, 1990), p. 132.

9. Ibid.; Gary Sick, *All Fall Down: America's Fateful Encounter with Iran* (London: I.B. Tauris, 1985), p. 197.

10. Baqer Moin, *Khomeini: Life of the Ayatollah* (London: I.B. Tauris, 1999), p. 227.

11. Bahman Baktiari, *Parliamentary Politics in Revolutionary Iran* (Gainesville: University Press of Florida, 1996), p. 70.

12. Menashri, *Iran: A Decade of War and Revolution,* p. 132.

13. Ibid., p. 147; Moin, pp. 220–221.

14. Baktiari, p. 59.

15. Ibid., p. 69.

16. Charles M. Sennott, "Hostage-Takers Rethink Their Role," *Boston Globe,* October 31, 1999, p. E1; Sandro Contenta, "Former Rebels in Iran Turn Backs on 1979," *Toronto Star,* October 23, 1999.

17. The Hujjatiyyah Society and post-Revolution parliamentary faction should not be confused with the Hujjatiyyah Seminary in Qum, a school founded by Ayatollah Muhammad Hujjat and later turned by Ayatollah Husayn 'Ali Montazeri into a mechanism for exporting the Islamic Revolution through education. See Farhang Rajaee, "Iranian Ideology and Worldview: The Cultural Export of Revolution," in *The Iranian Revolution: Its Global Impact,* ed. John Esposito (Miami: Florida International University Press, 1990), pp. 74–75.

18. Moin, pp. 66–67.

19. Menashri, *Iran: A Decade of War and Revolution,* pp. 220–222; Baktiari, p. 82.

20. John Kifner, "Khomeini Faction Challenged by More Conservative Group," *New York Times,* April 13, 1982, p. A1.

21. "Hanging Heretics,"*Economist,* June 25, 1983, p. 51.

22. David Menashri, "Iran," in *Middle East Contemporary Survey,* vol. 7: 1982–1983, ed. Colin Legum et al. (New York: Holmes & Meier Publishers, 1985), pp. 520–521; Baktiari, p. 95.

23. For examples of Hujjatiyyah appearing in political discourse, see "Text of Khomeyni Message to Teachers, Students," *Tehran Domestic Service,*

February 23, 1989, in FBIS-NES-89-036, February 24, 1989, p. 61; Asgar Schirazi, *The Constitution of Iran: Politics and the State in the Islamic Republic,* trans. John O'Kane (London: I.B. Tauris, 1997), p. 129; Baktiari, p. 233.

24. Masud Kuhistani Nijad, "Introducing the Islamic Mo'talefeh [Coalition] Association [An interview with Mr. Habibollah Asgar Owladi]," *Guzaresh,* no. 93, October 1998, online at www.netiran.com/Htdocs/Clippings/DPolitics/981022XXDP01.htm

25. Shahrokh Vaziri, "Les Groupes Dominants et le Jeu Politique Islamique en Iran" (Dominant groups and the Islamic political game in Iran) *Les Cahiers du CEDI* (Lausanne, Switzerland: Centre d'Etude et de Documentation Iraniennes, 2000), p. 6.

26. "Iran: Leader of Political Group Calls on All Factions to Unite," Islamic Republic News Agency (IRNA), December 27, 1998, in BBC Worldwide Monitoring, December 28, 1988.

27. Vaziri, p. 6.

28. Nijad, "Introducing the Islamic Mo'talefeh [Coalition] Association [An interview with Mr. Habibollah Asgar Owladi]."

29. "Head of Right-Wing Faction Calls for Probe of Press Role in Disturbances," *Iran,* July 19, 1999, in BBC Worldwide Monitoring, July 21, 1999 (ME/D3592/MED).

30. Vaziri, p. 6.

31. Abbas Samii, "Public Anger over Slow Pace of Prosecutions," RFE/RL *Iran Report* 2, no. 17, April 26, 1999.

32. Twelver Shi'ism, the predominant Islamic sect in Iran, holds that shortly before his death, the Prophet Muhammad appointed 'Ali as Imam, or leader of the faithful. From 'Ali, this position passed through twelve generations until the twelfth Imam, Muhammad al-Mahdi, disappeared in A.D. 874. At the end of the world, he will reappear as the Imam-i Zaman, the messiah, who will usher in the Day of Judgment. See J.J. Saunders, *A History of Medieval Islam* (London: Routledge, 1993), p. 127.

33. Samii,"Public Anger over Slow Pace of Prosecutions."

34. Ayatollah Milani was a senior Shi'i source of emulation *(marja'-i taqlid)* who interceded with the shah's government in 1963 to spare Khomeini the death penalty. See Shaul Bakhash, *The Reign of the Ayatollahs: Iran and the Islamic Revolution* (London: I.B. Tauris and Company, 1985), p. 30.

35. "Mahdaviyat Group behind Razini's Aborted Assassination Attempt," IRNA, April 24, 1999. See also the mention of Guardian Council cleri-

cal member Ayatullah Abulqasim Khaz'ali speaking before the ICA in 1996 in "Senior Cleric Defends Iran's System of Government against 'Apostate' Critics," *Resalat,* July 10, 1996, in BBC Summary of World Broadcasts, July 17, 1996 (EE/D2666/MF).

36. "Iran 'Crushed' Group Planning Assassination of Khatami," IRNA, November 25, 1999, in FBIS-NES-1999-1125.

37. Ibid.

38. Abbas Samii, "Mahdaviyyat Group Another Scapegoat," RFE/RL *Iran Report* 2, no. 47, November 29, 1999.

39. *World Fact Book* (Washington, DC: Central Intelligence Agency, 1999), online at www.cia.gov/cia/publications/factbook/ir.html#people; *Iran Statistical Yearbook 1376 [March 1997–March 1998]* (Tehran: Statistical Centre of Iran, 1998), p. 68, and previous editions.

40. "Confrontation Noted in Zahedan," IRNA, February 1, 1994, in FBIS-NES-94-023, February 3, 1994, p. 39; "Authorities Admit to Disturbances in Southeast," *al-Hayat,* February 3, 1994, in FBIS-NES-94-024, February 4, 1994, p. 37.

41. Although the Islamic Republic did not publicly blame the Sunnis, "unity" declarations hinted at their involvement. See "Muslims Stage Unity Demonstration in Zahedan," Voice of the Islamic Republic of Iran, February 6, 1994, in FBIS-NES-94-025, February 7, 1994, p. 66; "Sunni Leaders Condemn Presidential Assassination Bid," IRNA, February 6, 1994, in FBIS-NES-94-025, February 7, 1994, p. 66; Colin Barraclough, "Violence, Economic Woes Leave Iranian Revolution at Low Ebb," *San Francisco Chronicle,* July 13, 1994, p. A10; Wilfried Buchta, *Who Rules Iran? The Structure of Power in the Islamic Republic* (Washington, DC: The Washington Institute for Near East Policy and Konrad Adenauer Stiftung, 2000), p. 108.

42. Kenneth Katzman, *The Warriors of Islam: Iran's Revolutionary Guard* (Boulder, Colorado: Westview Press, 1993), p. 150.

43. "Iran Executes Former Head of Global Islamic Movement," Associated Press, September 28, 1987.

44. Menashri, *Iran: A Decade of War and Revolution,* pp. 23–24.

45. Katzman, pp. 3, 99; Baktiari, p. 133. Robin Wright refers to the organization as the World Islamic Movement; see Robin Wright, *In the Name of God: The Khomeini Decade* (New York: Touchstone, 1989), p. 139. Anthony Cordesman and Ahmed Hashim refer to it as the Organization for the Liberation of Revolutionary Fighters; see Anthony Cordesman and Ahmed Hashim, *Iran: Dilemma of Dual Containment* (Boulder: Westview Press, 1997), p. 148.

46. Moin, p. 264.

47. Mohammad-Reza Djalili, *Diplomatie Islamique: Stratégie Internationale du Khomeynisme* (Islamic diplomacy: the international strategy of Khomeinism) (Paris: Presses Universitaires de France, 1989), pp. 181–182; Menashri, *Iran: A Decade of War and Revolution,* p. 366.

48. "Foreign News Briefs," United Press International, August 25, 1986; "Prime Minister's Warning to Saudi Government on Hajj Arrests," IRNA in English, August 27, 1986, in BBC Summary of World Broadcasts, December 16, 1986 (ME/8348/A/1).

49. Michael Dunn, "Until the Imam Comes: Iran Exports Its Revolution," *Defense and Foreign Affairs,* July/August 1987, p. 43.

50. Louis Fares, "Syrian Diplomat Kidnapped in Tehran, Then Freed," Associated Press, October 3, 1986.

51. James Bill, *The Eagle and the Lion: The Tragedy of American–Iranian Relations* (New Haven: Yale University Press, 1988), pp. 1–3.

52. Baktiari, p. 135.

53. Ibid., p. 133.

54. Nora Boustany, "Beirut Magazine Says McFarlane Secretly Visited Tehran," *Washington Post,* November 4, 1986, p. A15.

55. Stanley Reed, "'Beirut Rag': *Al Shiraa* magazine," *The Nation,* December 20, 1986, p. 692.

56. Moin, p. 264.

57. Rafsanjani's role in the arrests is based on diplomatic sources cited in "Iran Executes Former Head of Global Islamic Movement," Associated Press, September 28, 1987. Intelligence Minister Muhammad Rayshari denied that the Iran–Contra leak and Hashemi's arrest were related. See "Iranian Information Minister on British Spies, Background to Hashemi Case," IRNA in English, December 14, 1986, in BBC Summary of World Broadcasts, December 16, 1986 (ME/8443/A/1).

58. Dunn, p. 43.

59. Ahmad Khomeini, *Ranjnameh* (A book of suffering) (n.p, n.d.), pp. 42–43, as quoted in Moin, p. 292.

60. Ibid.

61. Muhammad Rayshahri, *Khaterat* (Tehran: Center for Research, 1991), p. 28, as cited in Baktiari, pp. 133–134.

62. "Iranian Information Minister on British Spies, Background to Hashemi Case."

63. Ibid.

64. Ed Blanche, "Firing Squad Executes Former Aide to Khomeini's Successor," Associated Press, September 28, 1987.

65. Baktiari, p. 171; Buchta, pp. 81–82.

66. Schirazi, p. 129. Moin includes the text of letters exchanged between Khomeini and Montazeri (pp. 287–290).

67. "Reyshahri, Mohtashami Respond to Ahmad Montazeri," *Tehran Times*, August 31, 1999.

68. "Followers of Leading Cleric Close Down Iranian Town in Protest," Associated Press, April 25, 1998; Afshin Valinejad, "Hard-Liners Turn out at Prayer Service to Thwart Rally in Support of Dissident," Associated Press, May 15, 1998.

69. "Followers of Leading Cleric Close Down Iranian Town in Protest."

70. "Wave of Arrests in Dissident Iranian Cleric's Hometown," Agence France Presse, May 18, 1998.

71. Abbas Samii, "Mehdi Hashemi or Scapegoats?" RFE/RL *Iran Report* 2, no. 3, January 18, 1999.

72. Abbas Samii, "Hardliners Still Fear Montazeri," RFE/RL *Iran Report* 2, no. 44, November 8, 1999.

73. Samii, "Mehdi Hashemi or Scapegoats?"

Chapter 3
Ansar-i Hizbullah: The Vigilante Group of the Hardline Masses

A t times of uncertainty and political crisis in Iran, numerous vigilante groups often operate simultaneously (See Table, p. xviii). The groups are generally composed of small, tightly knit cells that remain dependent upon the guidance of leading ideologues and the generosity of benefactors. During the 1905–1909 Constitutional Revolution, anjumans were organized at the local level in cities across Iran, their actions coordinated by telegraph. The Pahlavi monarchy likewise saw the operation of several religious pressure groups, each centered around a different clerical figure. Even during the 1979 Islamic Revolution, many groups rose and fell with the fortunes of their leading personalities.

Many of the pressure groups active in Iran today are actually descendants or reincarnations of previous groups. It can be said that the Hujjatiyyah of the 1950s spawned the Hujjatiyyah of the 1980s and perhaps even the Mahdaviyyat of the 1990s. Other groups, including Furqan, Students Following the Line of the Imam, and the Mehdi Hashemi Gang are relatively new. Among the more recently appearing vigilantes are the counterrevolutionary patrol groups, like *Sar-i Allah* (Vengeance of God) and the *Qari'a* (Calamity), formed by the Iranian government in 1983. Sar-i Allah eventually evolved into both the *Jund-i Allah* (Army of God), which carried out counterinsurgency and anti-smuggling operations in rural areas beginning around 1984, and the *Ansar-i Allah* (Defenders of God), which combated profiteering in the cities.[1] Because both of the latter units operated within the IRGC, they functioned in a more official capacity than did other pressure groups.[2]

44

Perhaps the most prominent of the new vigilante organizations to emerge in recent years, however, is a group known as *Ansar-i Hizbullah* (Defenders of the Party of God). Acting as "brownshirts" for the Islamic Republic's hardline fringe, Ansar-i Hizbullah members have created a name for themselves through their increasingly violent attacks on those toeing a more reformist line. Although the "Sa'id Imami Gang" and the more recent incarnation of Fida'iyan-i Islam (both of which are discussed in Chapter 4) function with an elite, clandestine membership, Ansar-i Hizbullah serves as the vigilante group "for the masses" despite its high-level sponsorship, recruiting from a pool of war veterans and Basij volunteer forces and using mob attack as its primary modus operandi.

Leadership, Structure, and Ideology

The hardline 'Ali Abbaspur, a University of California at Berkeley-trained nuclear physicist, former Majlis deputy from Tehran, and member currently of the Islamic Coalition Association, commented in a March 1998 interview that "Ansar-i Hizbullah is not just one group. There are tens of *hizbullahi* formations in Tehran."[3] "Hizbullahi," literally "one who follows the Party of God," is used in Iranian parlance to denote any hardliner. As such, there can be any number of "hizbullahi" groups, which need neither be formal political groups nor structured pressure groups like Ansar-i Hizbullah. Although Ansar-i Hizbullah might be a convenient umbrella front for any number of these loosely connected or even independent cells, its operations have shown the group to be structured, well financed, and well connected.[4]

At present, Masud Dehnamaki and Husayn Allah-Karam are the group's clear leaders, and Guardian Council chairman Ayatollah Ahmad Jannati is Ansar-i Hizbullah's chief patron. Dehnamaki, who edits the group's main newspaper, *Jebheh*, is perhaps the chief ideologue of the movement. Born around 1969, he was ten years old during the Islamic Revolution and sixteen when he went to the Iraqi front. He expressed his disdain for those who shun violence by attending the funeral of Sa'id Imami, the alleged mastermind of the 1998 dissident murders,[5] and he maintains an open grudge against the West. In August 1999, Dehnamaki granted an interview to a Western correspondent in which he explained, "Western states sold chemicals to Iraq to attack us. Then they deliberately sold us faulty gas masks." He claimed to be present in Halabja, an Iraqi Kurdish town close to the Iranian border, when Iraqi forces used poison gas on Iranian troops.[6] Samples of the supposedly faulty gas masks hang in his office as "a symbol of Western perfidy," while sandbags, steel helmets, and ammunition cases also decorate the walls as a reminder of the militaristic values of the Islamic Republic during the Iran–Iraq War—a time in which dissent from within the Islamic government was tantamount to treason.[7]

Husayn Allah-Karam often acts as a spokesman for Ansar-i Hizbullah. A war veteran like Dehnamaki, Allah-Karam pursued a doctorate in management from Tehran University and continues to serve in the IRGC, reportedly as a brigadier-general.[8] Amir Farshad Ibrahimi, a self-described former operative in the group and the former head of the Islamic Union of Hizbullah Students, has identified Allah-Karam as having served in the Quds forces of the Revolutionary Guards during the war in Bosnia, and reported that Allah-Karam returned to Bosnia to manage a travel agency used by the IRGC as a cover for its own operations and espionage.[9]

Several hardline theorists have been identified as contributors to Ansar-i Hizbullah's intellectual leadership, including Husayn Shari'atmadari, Mehdi Nasiri, Yusifali Mir-Shakkak, Shahriar Zarshinas, Ahmad Fardid, and Riza Davari.[10] Dehnamaki's aide, Suhayl Karimi, and newspaper publisher Ahmad Kazemzadeh also play key intellectual roles. Ibrahimi has claimed that Bakhshi Kudzuri and religious hardliner Hojjatolislam Parvazi helped Allah-Karam and Dehnamaki to co-found the group, although Parvazi is said to have since broken off from it.[11] Together, Ansar-i Hizbullah's intellectual leaders propound an ideology that stresses loyalty to the values of the early revolutionary years, unquestioning allegiance to the Supreme Leader, strict religious observance, austerity, and xenophobic nationalism, shaped largely by the Iran–Iraq War and a provincial upbringing. Despite its virulent anti-Americanism, Ansar-i Hizbullah has managed to remain focused on combating domestic reformers, although at any time the group could shift its strategy to the targeting of Westerners.

Official and Popular Support

Like Fida'iyan-i Islam and the Hujjatiyyah before it, Ansar-i Hizbullah enjoys high-level tolerance and sponsorship. Ibrahimi recently alleged that the ICA transferred "huge amounts of money" to the group to fund its operations.[12] Influential ICA secretary-general Habibullah Asgarawladi, however, has denied such support, notwithstanding his praise for Ansar-i Hizbullah activities.[13] Hamid Najjari, secretary of the Assembly of the Party of God (*Majma'-i Hizbullah*), a formal parliamentary coalition, also consistently praises the group.

Ansar-i Hizbullah's highest-ranking open supporter may be Ahmad Jannati. Appointed to the Council of Guardians by Ayatollah Ruhollah Khomeini in 1980, Jannati now chairs that powerful body. Additionally, he sits on the Expediency Council (the clerical body that arbitrates disputes between the Majlis and the Guardian Council), and directs the Islamic Propagation Organization, an extremely hardline propaganda wing of the Islamic Republic, responsible for printing some of the most virulently anti-Western and anti-Semitic tracts in Iran. Lastly, he frequently serves as substitute Friday prayer leader in Tehran—the Islamic Republic's most prominent state-sponsored soapbox. Clearly, holding so many powerful and trusted positions, Jannati has Supreme Leader 'Ali Khamene'i's ear. In December 1998, the London-based Arabic monthly *al-Mujaz'an Iran* published a speech by self-described Ansar-i Hizbullah member Parvazi (who allegedly defected from the group), in which Parvazi labeled Jannati as "the father of the party's spirit."[14] And Jannati himself once declared, "If the Hizbullah are confronted with a moral vice, and if the Judiciary does not take necessary action to stop it, they can act on their own accord and the judicial authorities do not have the right to pursue them."[15] In an interview with the *Tehran Times*, Jannati denied official ties to the group but expressed his support for "any pure movement aiming to safeguard the Islamic values and ideals." In the same interview, he denounced "the deceitful propaganda campaign launched by the global arrogance [the United States], the Zionist regime, and certain mass media against Hizbullah forces inside the country [Iran]."[16]

Among the ruling elite, Jannati is perhaps the most reactionary and anti-Western. His pronouncements make clear that he considers the values of the Islamic Revolution to be immutable, and his record suggests that he would view any relaxation of social and political codes, along with any diplomatic rapprochement with the United States, as treasonous.[17] While leading Friday prayers in November 1992, Jannati announced, "We should not be afraid of making our intention known to the world . . . that we will mobilize the zealous vigilantes against the West and against the seekers of unjust domination."[18] Following a November 1998 Fida'iyan-i Islam attack on a busload of American visitors (See Chapter 4), Jannati again used the occasion of Friday prayers to declare, "Any Americans who come to Iran should be viewed with suspicion. We must be very cautious about allowing even Americans who come as tourists into Iran."[19] Jannati is equally hostile to Iranian reformists, whom he sees as betrayers of the Islamic Revolution. In an explosive videotaped confession in 2000 regarding his own role in Ansar-i Hizbullah (a confession disputed by the Iranian government), Amir Farshad Ibrahimi alleged that Jannati provided the group with funds to pursue common objectives against reformers and Westernizers.

In that videotaped statement, Ibrahimi also claimed that *Kargazaran-i Sazandigi* (Servants of Reconstruction), the political faction centered around Hashemi Rafsanjani, had assisted in forming Ansar-i Hizbullah on the orders of Rafsanjani during his presidency (1989–1997).[20] Ibrahimi reported that it was a temporary alliance with Rafsanjani that led to Parvazi's defection from the group. He claimed that Rafsanjani and Ghulamhusayn Karbaschi, a prominent reformist and the former mayor of Tehran, planned to use the group to "attack" themselves and their political allies in order to boost their own reformist credentials; Parvazi, on the other hand, claimed he would not do anything that would help a politician like Rafsanjani who often placed self-promotion above ideology.[21] Although there is little evidence to support these allegations, if true they would only confirm the pattern by which Iranian officials create and use vigilante groups to further their own objectives, only to lose control of those groups as the vigilantes radicalize and become more violent.

In his confession, Ibrahimi detailed more alleged high-level connections to Ansar-i Hizbullah. He said that Supreme Leader Ali Khamene'i once summoned the group's leaders (an incident confirmed by Parvazi) and reportedly expressed displeasure at their decision to continue with the use of violence.[22] The mere act of receiving an invitation to meet with the Supreme Leader can be seen as an endorsement, however, especially for those not officially part of the government apparatus. Ibrahimi claimed that Ansar-i Hizbullah members later received encouragement from Habibullah Asgarawladi and hardline theoretician Ayatollah Misbah-Yazdi,[23] and he fingered Qum-based hardliner Ayatollah Nuri Hamadani as another prominent supporter and instigator of Ansar-i Hizbullah activities.[24] Parvazi once reported that Ansar-i Hizbullah also received support from Ahmad Mir-Hijazi, former deputy intelligence minister and one of only four senior members of the Office of the Supreme Leader.[25]

In 1998, the liberal journal *Iran-i Farda,* a target of repeated Ansar-i Hizbullah attacks, reported that the pressure group was receiving financial backing from one of Iran's largest revolutionary foundations, the Foundation for the Oppressed and Disabled.[26] The revolutionary foundations operate vast corporate empires, often with property and funds that were confiscated from the shah, his allies, and wealthy regime opponents, along with Western property nationalized during the Islamic Revolution. Supreme Leader Khamene'i appoints foundation heads who remain subservient to few but Khamene'i himself. Accordingly, Iran's revolutionary foundations have become channels through which hard currency and equipment can be funneled to a variety of Iranian hardliner causes.[27] In a 1995 interview, Muhsin Rafiq-Dust, former commander of the IRGC and then-chairman of the Foundation for the Oppressed and Disabled, claimed that his foundation controlled business and property worth $10 billion.[28] This foundation is heavily involved in Iran's travel industry and operates not only travel agencies but also many Iranian hotels. In a 1998 report, *Iran-i Farda* editor and noted reformist 'Izzatullah Sahabi specifically alleged that Ansar-i Hizbullah leader Husayn Allah-Karam was receiving funds laundered through one of these foundation-controlled travel agencies.[29]

Although Ansar-i Hizbullah apparently relies on high-level patronage, the group's core is its anti-intellectual rank and file. Most of its current members were too young to have participated in the Islamic Revolution, and thus they saw their service in the Iran–Iraq War as an opportunity to take part in "the revolutionary epic." During the war period, they came to extol Ayatollah Khomeini in all the revolutionary mythology that developed around him. Indeed, the Ayatollah possessed not only spiritual authority and incredible charisma but also a class background similar to their own.[30] At the end of the war, however, veterans returning to their cities felt that they were receiving insufficient respect for their sacrifice, while many of those in power were conspicuously well fed, wore Western-style clothes, and drove the latest-model cars. Corruption was rampant, and the veterans saw that many government officials appeared to be enjoying life without significant sacrifice.[31] As Iranian writer Muhammad Quchani explains, "Preachers were sanctifying private ownership from the pulpits. Rich bazaar merchants were strutting so elegantly and haughtily in supermarkets that they had even forgotten to calculate their *khums* (tax earmarked for the needy) and *zakat* (alms)."[32] Moreover, while officials were vilifying the

United States in the strongest of terms, Iran had actually increased its volume of trade with "the Great Satan" during the war period and seemed no longer to be making any real attempt to export the revolution.[33] Obviously, not every frustrated veteran joined a radical pressure group to vent his anger, but a dispossessed core did form out of this post-war malaise and disillusionment.

Quchani (himself arrested and detained without trial in August 2000), has theorized that Ansar-i Hizbullah's anti-intellectual bent also had roots in the strength of the bazaaris during the Islamic Revolution. He explains that the clergy in the early years of the Islamic Republic "advocated conservative economic policies [and] defended cultural radicalism. Instead of arousing young people against the capitalists, they incited them against women and intellectuals."[34] Even during the heyday of the Islamic Revolution and the ensuing Iran–Iraq War, Iranian authorities knew that they could not risk antagonizing the bazaaris, whose religious conservatism and social traditionalism had made them a backbone of the Islamic Revolution. Women and intellectuals, in their thinking, did not merit such protection.

Operational Doctrine

Ansar-i Hizbullah operations would be impossible to carry out without high-level backing; in the absence of such support, the group could not continue to publish its incendiary newspaper or successfully keep its rank and file out of prison for their extremist activities. But the effectiveness and resilience of Ansar-i Hizbullah are also attributable to the group's small size and its access to money and equipment. Although no clear membership figures are available, Ansar-i Hizbullah's core probably includes no more than a few hundred members. As such, the cells remain tight and can operate by word of mouth.

According to one member of an Iranian regional interest group, pressure groups tend not to operate outside major cities because the IRGC and other security services can move more freely against their opponents away from the spotlight of the Western and Iranian press.[35] Nevertheless, Ansar-i Hizbullah is predominantly an urban organization. It is based in Tehran and also maintains a "chapter" in Isfahan, where the young seminary student Kumayl Kaveh leads the local group.[36] Vigilantes from Ansar-i Hizbullah have repeatedly harassed Isfahan's Friday prayer leader, whom they deem too sympathetic to Ayatollah Husayn 'Ali Montazeri and thus insufficiently loyal to the concept of *vilayat-i faqih* (Montazeri is perhaps the highest-ranking religious opponent of this concept). During the celebrations surrounding the full solar eclipse on August 11, 1999, vigilantes also attacked Italian and American tourists visiting Isfahan.[37]

Other Ansar-i Hizbullah activities seem to be organized through hardline university groups, such as the Islamic Union of Hizbullah Students.[38] Student unions in Iran are much more political and even influential than those in the United States. While the Islamic Union of Hizbullah Students is still relatively small, it remains extremely well supported and protected by hardline authorities. Moreover, although Iranian universities may be relative bastions of reform, many students still gain admittance based on their Islamist connections rather than their intellect, a reality that intimidates many professors.[39]

Ansar-i Hizbullah also appears to have ready access to equipment normally accessible only to the IRGC and the paramilitary Basij volunteer forces. For example, in April 2000, the reformist newspaper *'Asr-i Azadagan* reported that the group once maintained a depot in Shahr-i Rayy, where it secured access to a number of 1,000 cubic centimeter–engine motorcycles—vehicles ostensibly reserved only for the official security forces. Ansar-i Hizbullah members have apparently been permitted to procure those motorcycles at any time for use in their operations, such as drive-by attacks on cinemas and press offices.[40] Indeed, a key element in the modus operandi of Ansar-i Hizbullah is the frequent targeting of reformist newspapers. In January 1999, two suspected Ansar-i Hizbullah members riding by the offices of the pro-Khatami daily *Khurdad* lobbed a percussion grenade at the newspaper's offices, shattering windows and injuring some journalists. In 1999, when the Press Court announced the ban on *Zan* (Woman), the reformist newspaper run by Rafsanjani's daughter Fa'izeh, Dehnamaki declared that Fa'izeh should be executed. Somewhat ironically, the newspaper Dehnamaki edited at the time (*Shalamcheh*) was the next to be banned in the crackdown.[41]

The Role of the Media

At the same time, Ansar-i Hizbullah relies heavily upon the media to sustain a public presence and publicize its vision. In this regard, it maintains close relations with the widely circulated hardline daily *Kayhan* and the monthly *Subh*.[42] In a July 23, 2000, editorial, reformist newspaper *Bahar* lamented the fact that "a public newspaper [*Kayhan*] is totally placed at the disposal of the pressure groups for propaganda purposes and support."[43] Indeed, the Iranian media may well be considered a pillar of Ansar-i Hizbullah's success. While reformist newspapers tend to outnumber the hardline newspapers (at least in periods during which the reformist press is not subject to government closure), hardline newspapers tend to be more stable and have better access to resources, due to the patronage of high-level officials.

But Ansar-i Hizbullah maintains its own newspapers as well. Initially, Dehnamaki published and edited the weekly *Shalamcheh* (named after a battle during the Iran–Iraq War, the Iranian equivalent of the Alamo), which was shut down in February 1999 under pressure from individuals within Khatami's more moderate government. Just days later, Dehnamaki founded the nearly identical *Jebheh* (Front) but was prevented by the pro-Khatami Ministry of Culture and Islamic Guidance from holding the publishing license. Instead, Dehnamaki retained editorship but passed on the roles of publisher and managing director to Ahmad Kazimzadeh and Ahmad Kazimpur, respectively.[44] Other *Jebheh* staff members included Suhayl Karimi, a photographer, and Riza Monjizipur, a reporter.[45] Fatima Rajabi, Yusif Ghulam Riza, Muhammad Riza Qafali, Muhammad Malik, 'Abbas Nizari, and Sayyid Husayn Muhtahidi also published in *Jebheh* and are therefore presumably Ansar-i Hizbullah members.[46] In addition to the weekly, Abdulhamid Muhtasham publishes *Ya Litharat al-Husayn* (Vengeance of Husayn), edited by Bakhshi Kudzuri, which represents Ansar-i Hizbullah's more economically conservative faction.[47]

Jebheh itself had published just fifty-five issues before April 29, 2000, when it was closed as the "token" hardline newspaper among twenty reform newspapers and magazines in a hardline regime crackdown on the reform media.[48] Although it shared much material with hardline monthly *Subh, Jebheh* also published its own interviews and analysis. In addition, it was virulently critical of President Muhammad Khatami and his reformist allies, and of the policies of Expediency Council chairman and former president Rafsanjani.[49] Dehnamaki once explained that the newspaper's distinction was its ability to portray the hizbullahi point of view accurately in a journalistic milieu biased in favor of reformers. After *Jebheh*'s closure, Dehnamaki told an interviewer that "because the Hizbullah forces have never had an official forum, usually political factions are misusing their protests and statements. Newspapers will publish our words according to their own preferences and would either support or criticize us according to their own interests."[50] Although numerically, reformist newspapers outnumber hardline publications (in periods during which the hardline Judiciary does not ban the former), Dehnamaki's assertion indicates that he blames the press for creating reformism in Iran, rather than vice versa. Indeed, almost all visitors to Iran freely acknowledge that the Iranian public is generally far more progressive and Western looking than the theocratic government.

But *Jebheh,* and *Shalamcheh* before it, went beyond simply casting the radical hizbullahis in a favorable light. Rather, they focused hardline attention on specific reformist and dissident targets. For example, the Press Court (the sector of the Judiciary that handles press affairs) canceled *Shalamcheh*'s license after it accused the late Grand Ayatollah Abulqasim al-Khu'i of working for the shah's secret police.[51] Despite Khu'i's religious credentials (he held a higher rank in the religious hierarchy before his death in 1992 than Supreme Leader Khamene'i currently holds), he disagreed with the idea of vilayat-i faqih, the principle of clerical rule blindly protected by Ansar-i Hizbullah. Khu'i disagreed with Khomeini and Khamene'i in this regard, but in slandering such a high-ranking religious official, *Shalamcheh* had pushed even the hardline Judiciary too far.

In another instance, on August 16, 1997, three days before the hardline-dominated Majlis began debating President Khatami's nominations for cabinet posts, five suspected Ansar-i Hizbullah vigilantes attacked the office and staff of the reformist *Iran-i Farda* magazine. Just before the attack, *Shalamcheh* had strongly criticized the magazine for publishing an article that questioned the institution of obligatory prayer in government offices. The pro-Khatami Ministry of Culture and Islamic Guidance strongly condemned the attack, declaring, "This kind of action will lead to anarchy and benefit the enemies of the revolution."[52] *Shalamcheh* had published its criticism, however, not merely to condemn a viewpoint with which its publishers disagreed, but also to focus the attention of Ansar-i Hizbullah vigilantes on the prayer issue at a time when reformists were basking in the glow of Khatami's inauguration and celebrating the ouster of many old-guard hardliners from the presidential cabinet. It is the unstated but widely held belief of many Iranians that Dehnamaki received high-level government encouragement, if not outright orders, to target *Iran-i Farda*.

In early January 1998, *Shalamcheh* became much more direct in its attacks on Khatami. Responding to the latter's January 8, 1998, "address to the American people" aired on Cable News Network, *Shalamcheh* likened Khatami to Mehdi Bazargan, the Islamic Republic's first prime minister, forced from office for not taking a sufficiently hardline stance against the United States.[53] In apparent response to this pronouncement, Khatami soon toughened his rhetoric against Washington and the prospect of rapprochement, effectively demonstrating the influence that Ansar-i Hizbullah wielded in this circumstance.[54] More recently, on September 11, 1999, *Shalamcheh*'s successor, *Jebheh*, offered to donate 100 million rials (approximately $33,000) for the "revolutionary execution" of Husayn Baqirzadeh, a London-based human rights activist, provided that a senior cleric issue a *fatwa* (religious edict) justifying his execution.[55]

Dehnamaki himself was seen at the July 9, 1999, vigilante attack on students at the Tehran University dormitory (described below), but he claims only to have been present in his capacity as a reporter for *Jebheh*.[56] He did not explain how he knew of the attack in advance. In November 1999, Dehnamaki told *Subh-i Imruz* that his next goal would be to effect the dismissal of Minister of Culture and Islamic Guidance Ata'ullah Muhajarani, a prominent reformist ally of Khatami.[57] Later, on May 5, 2000 (after the ban was announced but too late to preclude the distribution of its last issue), *Jebheh* published a fatwa authorizing the murder of Davud Nimati, an Iranian exile and German-language editor of Salman Rushdie's *Satanic Verses*, a book condemned by Ayatollah Khomeini in 1989.[58]

Notwithstanding the impact of these hardline activities, neither *Shalamcheh/Jebheh* nor Ansar-i Hizbullah can be presumed to be mouthpieces for Iran's mainstream, traditionalist right wing; rather, they must be construed as representing the most extreme conservative interests in the Islamic Republic. In a series of articles leading up to parliamentary elections, *Jebheh* sought to distance itself from its more traditionalist hardline base. Serving as an indicator of Ansar-i Hizbullah's radicalization, *Jebheh* argued in the fall of 1999 that the presence in Ansar-i Hizbullah of such figures as Husayn Shari'atmadari, executive editor of the hardline newspaper *Kayhan*, would damage the group's credibility. In a later article, *Jebheh* wrote that, with the increasing factionalism in Iranian politics, neither the Second of Khurdad (reformist) movement nor the "rightist" faction could represent "the true interest of the government." Rather, *Jebheh* argued, Hizbullah (in this context meaning the more extreme ideological hardliners rather than the formalized hizbullahis of the government parliamentary factions) had formed a base for a third force, "the Third Revolutionary Line," dedicated to faith "in the pure Islam of Muhammad."[59]

According to Dehnamaki, *Jebheh*'s circulation fluctuated between 70,000 and 100,000 before its closure.[60] Although his estimate may be exaggerated, such a large readership cannot be ruled out. In his capacity as representative of a political movement and a point of view convenient to high-ranking officials that may have included even the Supreme Leader himself, Dehnamaki may very well have received funds to subsidize the newspaper.

A History of Violent Intimidation

In a speech delivered to hardline paramilitary Basij members on the occasion of Muhammad Khatami's 1997 election, Hojjatolislam Parvazi traced Ansar-i Hizbullah's roots to a group calling itself *Razmandigan* (Warriors), formed in 1984, to which he belonged. Because of the immediacy of problems concerning the Iran–Iraq War, however, Parvazi said that the group remained inactive; the Islamic Republic was fighting for survival after the Iraq invasion, and quibbles over ideology therefore took a back seat. With the end of the war in 1988, Parvazi and the late Sayyid 'Ali Najafi apparently moved the group to Tehran and began to recruit others.[61] Masud Dehnamaki told *Haftehnameh-yi Siyasat* (Policy Weekly) that Ansar-i Hizbullah began acting as a distinct group in 1989, although it did not adopt its name until 1993 and did not become recognizably distinct until 1995.[62]

Eighteen men constituted the membership of Ansar-i Hizbullah at the time of the group's renaming and rebirth. Seven of the original participants were followers of "one of the most prominent right-wing individuals who served in one of the most important and most powerful organizations in the country."[63] Another seven were nonclerical supporters of Iran's traditionalist right wing. The remaining four members, led by Husayn Allah-Karam, were a bit more leftist than the others, distrusting the free-market capitalism of many in the bazaari class.[64] The nascent pressure group reportedly had close relations with the IRGC and with the powerful Association of Instructors of Qum Religious Seminaries (*Jama'i Mudarrisin-i Hawzeh-yi 'Ilmiyeh-yi Qum*), which consisted of twenty-three high-ranking clerics. Both of these institutions were bastions of the traditionalist right.[65]

Ansar-i Hizbullah quickly earned a reputation for violence and also for apparent immunity from any legal prosecution. Hizbullahis, often no more than loosely organized religious street gangs, sought to impose their own views of morality on the streets of Iranian cities throughout the 1980s and 1990s. Ansar-i Hizbullah, however, inaugurated its own brand of vigilantism with a vengeance. In April 1995, vigilantes assaulted Islamic philosopher Abdulkarim Sorush as he prepared to give a lecture at the University of Isfahan.[66] Sorush, who studied philosophy in London, was known for disputing the clergy's claim to be the sole interpreters of Islam—an argument the latter use to justify their rule. In July 1995, hardline vigilantes disrupted the funeral service for Karim Sanjabi, a member of both the National Front (the former pro-Musaddiq party) and, later, the Mehdi Bazargan government. Crowds swelled to "several thousand" on the streets outside the Safi 'Alishah monastery where the funeral was being held, but the police mysteriously did not arrive for several hours. According to *Kayhan*, "Their absence was interpreted to mean that they wanted to give the semi-governmental hizbullahis a free hand to break up the ceremony."[67] In September 1995, vigilantes burned down a bookstore that stocked material they deemed too "liberal,"[68] and again authorities made no arrests. While news reports did not immediately specify that these attacks were the work of Ansar-i Hizbullah, it is likely that the sudden burst of hardline vigilantism in 1995 was a direct result of the activity of its members.

On October 11, 1995, chanting "death to opponents of vilayat-i faqih," assailants described initially just as "hizbullahis" disrupted another lecture by Sorush. Wielding clubs, the vigilantes struck Sorush and then proceeded to beat students in the audience, while chanting to drown out Sorush's lecture. *Salam* reported the incident at length in the next day's edition.[69] On October 14, the Islamic Society of Students (ISS) of Tehran University's technical department issued a statement in *Salam* declaring that the "conflict was completely one-sided, with a group of uninformed friends on one side and the organizers of the meeting . . . on the other." The ISS alleged in their statement that they had met with an official of Ansar-i Hizbullah before the event, a meeting in which the two sides agreed that Ansar-i Hizbullah would not interrupt Sorush's lecture and that the ISS would even provide another forum for Ansar-i Hizbullah members to speak.

In the midst of the mêlée, Dehnamaki himself took a bullhorn and demanded the opportunity to debate Sorush. He announced that until the philosopher so agreed, Ansar-i Hizbullah would continue to disrupt every Sorush event. (Dehnamaki's actions were reminiscent of Navvab-i Safavi's dogged pursuit of Ahmad Kasravi before Fida'iyan-i Islam operatives killed the author [See Chapter 1].[70]) On October 16, Dehnamaki hotly denied this account of the event and pronounced in an interview with *Salam* that "the assault was not in any way premeditated." Instead, he charged that the students had provoked Ansar-i Hizbullah activists. He also claimed that the organizers of the speech had tried to prevent the entrance of anyone looking religious, even though several of the Ansar-i Hizbullah members were registered students.[71]

But the debate surrounding this incident was not limited to the pages of the reformist *Salam*. As residents of Tehran bought their newspapers and rushed to work on October 24, 1995, they were greeted by full-page manifestos in several dailies declaring Ansar-i Hizbullah's resolve to expose financial corruption, stave off the cultural assault of the West, resist capitalism, crush liberalism and secular thought, and destroy those who advocated rapprochement with the United States. Itself evidence of considerable financial backing, this very public declaration was an unprecedented move for an Iranian pressure group. The manifesto declared, "Until our throats be cut, we will fight the supporters of the West and of anti-fundamentalist tendencies." Declaring no allegiance to any laws but those of God and responding forcefully to those who accused the group of illegal actions, the statement rhetorically asked, "Was the revolution itself a legal act? Was taking the nest of spies [the U.S. embassy] a legal act? Was handing over Israel's embassy to the Palestinians a legal act?"[72]

The October 1995 clash between Ansar-i Hizbullah vigilantes and students at Tehran University was not a one-time occurrence. Rather, the group has continued to focus attacks on Abdulkarim Sorush. A partial list of incidents follows:

- May 12, 1996: *Amir Kabir University, Tehran.* Sorush was forced to cancel a speech when 100 Ansar-i Hizbullah members surrounded the lecture hall. An Ansar-i Hizbullah activist declared that if ISS members "persist in their conspiracies, they will be hanged."[73]
- November 15, 1997: *Amir Kabir University, Tehran.* A mob of between 100 and 200 Ansar-i Hizbullah vigilantes led by Husayn Allah-Karam disrupted another planned lecture by Sorush at Amir Kabir University when they intercepted Sorush's car.[74]
- July 29, 1999: *Mashhad.* Vigilantes attacked Sorush at the conclusion of a talk that he gave in a private residence.
- October 18, 1999: *Tehran University.* The university canceled Sorush's philosophy classes because of vigilante threats to set fire to his classrooms.
- January 14, 2000: *Mashhad.* Vigilantes attacked Sorush's car, forcing him to cancel a lecture.[75]
- June 20, 2000: *Shiraz University.* A lecture hall in the university's literature faculty was burned down after Sorush delivered a lecture there.[76]
- August 27, 2000: *Khorrambad.* A student conference at which Sorush was to have spoken was cancelled when vigilantes blocked the entrance to the city's airport, leading to clashes and intervention by police and security forces.[77]

In the first half of 1996, vigilantes stepped up their intimidation campaign. During these months, Ansar-i Hizbullah raided weddings and private parties and attacked bicycle-riding women—whom some hardliners considered to be engaging in immodest behavior. On May 4, group members set fire to a movie theater in northern Tehran.[78] The following day the group struck again, targeting Tehran's popular *Quds* (Jerusalem) movie theater. Objecting to the screening of the comedy *Indian Gift*, approximately sixty vigilantes stormed the theater, beating employees and the audience, shattering windows, tearing posters, and smashing arcade games. Although the Ministry of Culture and Islamic Guidance had approved the film (cutting four minutes off a previously approved version in deference to Ansar-i Hizbullah objections), the group complained that a scene in which little boys and girls dance together joyously at a wedding ceremony held during the Iran–Iraq War years was obscene and disrespectful.[79]

Differing accounts report that at the movie theater, Allah-Karam made a declaration, and either Bakhshi Kudzuri (editor of Ansar i Hizbullah's *Ya Litharat al Husayn*) or a man named "Abdullahi" set the theater on fire.[80] Amir Farhad Ibrahimi, in his videotaped confession four years later, claimed that the deputy minister of culture and Islamic guidance, whose ministry was then under hardline control, summoned leading Ansar-i Hizbullah activists to reprimand them for the severity of their actions at the theater.[81] But far from apologizing for the violence, Ansar-i Hizbullah activist Dehnamaki chided the government for failing "to stop social problems and corruption."

In the same time period, Ansar-i Hizbullah also actively sought to intimidate reformists in the Fifth Majlis of the Islamic Republic (elected in March 1996), announcing that group members would seek to block reformers from taking their seats in the new parliament. Ahmad Jannati, as a senior political supporter of Ansar-i Hizbullah, declared that the group was "above the law and government institutions," explaining that "our revolution belongs to Hizbullah, and the time has come for the party to confront the enemies who have infiltrated the institutions to destroy the revolution."[82]

Ansar-i Hizbullah also targeted the foreign community in Iran as a way of consolidating hardline support. On April 11, 1997, a Berlin Court issued a guilty verdict in the "Mykonos trial," implicating Supreme Leader 'Ali Khamene'i, former President Rafsanjani, former Minister of Intelligence 'Ali Fallahian, and Foreign Minister Ali Akbar Velayati in the assassination of three Kurdish dissidents and their translator on September 18, 1992, in the Mykonos restaurant near Berlin.[83] Ansar-i Hizbullah activists quickly gathered in front of the German Embassy in Tehran, where Allah-Karam declared before a group of almost 1,000 supporters, "One of our followers will strap a bomb to himself and blow up the embassy if Germany continues its accusations and hostile attitude against our leaders."[84]

Three days later, approximately 250 radical students clashed with police in front of the embassy. The students issued a statement declaring, "If ever the guide orders us, we will wage a holy war against the infidels and nothing will prevent us. We are the conquerors of spy nests."[85] The protests continued for more than a week, with Ansar-i Hizbullah repeating its bomb threat on April 18. On April 19, however, German foreign minister Klaus Kinkel agreed to accept Iranian government assurances of his fellow citizens' safety, explaining, "Since suicide commandos only seem to act on orders from the government . . . we will take the Iranian government at its word."[86]

Soon thereafter, individuals criticized by high-ranking hardline officials began to come under attack. For example, the day after Judiciary Chief Ayatollah Muhammad Yazdi criticized the reformist newspaper *Tus,* declaring that "the Islamic people of Iran will not tolerate insults and attacks against their beliefs and the Shi'ite clergy," unidentified vigilantes brutally beat the newspaper's editor, Mashallah Shamsulva'zin.[87] On September 4, 1998, the day after Supreme Leader Khamene'i spoke of the necessity of purging "deviationist interpretations" and "negative and destructive teachings of Western freedom," vigilantes physically attacked Abdullah Nuri, then vice president for social and developmental affairs, and Ata'ullah Muhajarani, minister of culture and Islamic guidance. Denying responsibility for these attacks, Ansar-i Hizbullah labeled the incidents "regrettable" and "suspicious," hinting that the reformists themselves sought to "arrange" such attacks in order to capitalize on "chaotic conditions."[88]

But no other groups claimed responsibility or indicated motive. Both in their denial and in their referring to Khamene'i's statements in their declaration, Ansar-i Hizbullah members created greater suspicion that they were seeking to escalate the power struggle to a new level by adding physical force to Khamene'i's rhetoric. In early January 1999, shortly after the Ministry of Intelligence admitted the culpability of some of its agents in the murder of several intellectuals, *ash-Sharq al-Awsat* (a London-based, pan-Arabic newspaper) reported that investigations had in fact linked Ansar-i Hizbullah to the attacks on Nuri and Muhajarani.[89] Moreover, in November 1999, Dehnamaki told the reformist paper *Subh-i Imruz* that he sought the dismissal of Muhajarani for following "policies that he knows are wrong."[90]

In early 1998, there was speculation that Ansar-i Hizbullah had pushed too far in violently countering the pro-Khatami reformists. Following the physical attack on a reformist cleric conducting Friday prayers in Isfahan, police arrested several vigilantes. In response, the Expediency Council publicly criticized Allah-Karam, declaring his actions "harmful to the revolution."[91] But Muhsin Riza'i, secretary of the Expediency Council and former commander of the IRGC, refused to condemn Allah-Karam's actions, declaring them to be "of a personal nature" having nothing to do with the IRGC, despite Allah-Karam's rank of brigadier general in the Revolutionary Guards.[92] Subsequently, London-based Iranian investigative journalist 'Ali Nurizadeh reported that both Riza'i and Yahya Rahim Safavi, Riza'i's successor at the helm of the IRGC, had close links with Ansar-i Hizbullah's inner circle.[93]

Years earlier, when Riza'i was still commander of the Revolutionary Guards, he received a complaint from the generally moderate Islamic Society of Amir Kabir Industrial University about the link between Ansar-i Hizbullah and the IRGC. In its letter, excerpted in *Salam* in October 1995, the Islamic Society charged that the presence of IRGC members in Ansar-i

Hizbullah "has strengthened the impression that the military institution of the IRGC has had direct presence in political processes contrary to the explicit directives of His Eminence Imam Khomeini."[94] According to Hojjatolislam Parvazi, Ansar-i Hizbullah members were also connected to the Intelligence Ministry and—at least before the inauguration of Muhammad Khatami as president (in other words, while Khatami was either a minister or simply not in power)—to the Ministries of Interior and Culture as well.[95]

Nothing, however, would propel Ansar-i Hizbullah into the international spotlight like the events of July 1999, in which vigilante action directed against students protesting the closure of a reformist newspaper quickly escalated into the bloodiest rioting to hit Iran in two decades.

Setting off a Storm: The Attack on Tehran University

At 10 p.m. on July 8, 1999, after a peaceful protest in front of Tehran's *Kargar-i Shumali* (North Worker) street sparked by the closure of reformist newspaper *Salam,* a group of several dozen students were attacked by stone-hurling Ansar-i Hizbullah vigilantes. In the early hours of the next morning, more vigilantes arrived in government-owned buses.[96] After a lull, Ansar-i Hizbullah members—wielding clubs, chains, and riot gear—joined with the newly dispatched Law Enforcement Forces (LEF) in storming central Tehran's Amirabad student dormitory at 4:00 a.m., breaking windows, setting rooms ablaze, and clubbing students in the process. One student later reported that vigilantes had killed up to nine students both with gunfire and by throwing students out of the dormitory's upper-story windows.[97]

That the Iranian government did not immediately appreciate the seriousness of the situation was apparent in state-controlled IRNA's report the next morning claiming that "the security forces have the situation under control."[98] In fact, they did not. Bloody clashes erupted in Tehran for six straight days as at least 10,000 students staged a pro-democracy sit-in at Tehran University. In open defiance, they clamored for Supreme Leader 'Ali Khamene'i to "take responsibility for what has happened" at the dormitory.[99] But the worst was yet to come. On July 12, students rampaged through central Tehran, burning tires, overturning light posts, and destroying buses and bus stops. Emboldened by their indignation at the actions of the vigilantes and the police, protestors set a police car and two motorcycles ablaze.[100] Some demonstrators blamed Khamene'i for Ansar-i Hizbullah's actions, chanting, "Ansar commits crimes, and the Leader supports them. Oh, Great Leader, shame on you."[101]

Security forces then drove pick-up trucks through town, firing tear gas and rounding up protesters. Vigilantes on motorcycles, widely suspected of being members of Ansar-i Hizbullah, attacked both protesters and innocent bystanders. Hours later, broken glass littered the street.[102] Unable to shield the public from the scale of the protests without losing credibility, Iranian state television showed footage of burned buses and uprooted street signs. Students bragged openly about trying to rip down the gates of the Interior Ministry. Protests erupted at universities and cities across Iran, and in an effort to check their spread, the government shut down Iran's entire cellular phone network. What began as a reaction to the violence of the vigilantes was evolving into a full-scale challenge to hardliners—not only outside the government, but inside as well. When *Hamshahri* reported that LEF and Ansar-i Hizbullah had also cooperated in attacking students at Tabriz University,[103] Masud Dehnamaki denied the charges.[104]

Supreme Leader Khamene'i later gave a special address about the incident, declaring to an audience of religious hardliners, "This bitter incident has broken my heart." He acknowledged public anger against him, and urged, "Even if things make you angry and they condemn me, even if they set fire to my picture, remain silent. Take no action until the day that the country needs it!"[105] He did not accept personal responsibility, however, and instead placed the blame on enemies like the United States, as the televised crowd chanted "Death to America." Khamene'i supporters did not have to wait long to take action. On July 14, hardliners staged a series of anti-student, pro-Khamene'i demonstrations in cities across

Iran. Iranian state television footage showed pro-government gatherings in Tehran and almost every provincial capital. (While the crowds were huge—several hundred thousand in Tehran alone—they were still not as large as those formed to celebrate Khatami's election, or even Iran's entry into the 1998 World Cup soccer tournament.)

On the surface, life returned to normal in Tehran within days of the rioting, although soldiers continued to block off Tehran University, and anti-student graffiti littered the capital.[106] Shops reopened, people crowded the bazaars, motorcyclists and taxis once again filled the streets, and young middle- and upper-class students—among the most Westward looking in Iranian society—flocked to the mountains north of Tehran where social mores are generally a bit more relaxed. But scars remained. University students complained that Khatami, who had remained quiet even at peak moments of the conflict—agreeing to defer to Khamene'i—had betrayed them by not speaking out in support of civil liberties. Others, more sympathetic to the president, countered that Khatami had no other choice once the demonstrations began to spin out of control. Other residents of northern Tehran who were old enough to remember the 1979 Revolution noted that the LEF, Basij forces (who also helped to quell the protests in the aftermath of the dormitory attack), and vigilantes had in truth not successfully suppressed the demonstrations; rather, they insisted, the students and their allies had voluntarily retreated because, regardless of political viewpoint, few Iranians wanted violence and all feared civil war.[107]

The demonstrations that followed Ansar-i Hizbullah's attack on the student dormitory illustrated to Khamene'i and the hardliners just how deep seated popular dissatisfaction with the regime really was. Indeed, the hardliners could no longer pretend that Khatami's election was a fluke—a realization later reinforced by the dominance of Islamic Iran Participation Party (Iran's primary reform party) candidates and other reformist contenders in the Majlis elections of February 2000. At the same time, however, students, academics, taxi drivers, and storekeepers in Tehran, Isfahan, and Kirman clearly felt that the hardliners had won this round. *Salam* remained closed, hundreds of high school and university students languished in prison, and hardliners were able to cite national security concerns to justify increasing the presence of hardline security forces on the streets. The clear lesson for vigilante groups like Ansar-i Hizbullah was that no matter how strong the popular feeling to the contrary, a manufactured crisis could provide an excuse for the further erosion of civil liberty and reform.

The Investigation Begins

Although Khatami and Khamene'i, in effect, had cooperated both during and after the riots, the power struggle between the reform and hardline factions, respectively, with whom each was associated, continued behind the scenes. On July 17, 1999, Iranian state television broadcast an interview with Ghulamhusayn Bulandian, deputy interior minister for security affairs, and Muhsin Riza'i, who had by then become Tehran's deputy governor-general for political and security affairs.

Riza'i sought to diminish the implications of the police action during the riots by noting that the students of the Amirabad dormitory had, on several previous occasions, protested without a license. He did admit that "civilians" were working along with the LEF to quell the rioting, but insisted that they had coordinated their actions—inadvertently implying that government hardliners had been maintaining connections with Ansar-i Hizbullah. Asked directly whether the civilians were associated with Ansar-i Hizbullah, he responded, "Well, I did not identify them." Riza'i denied that any LEF troops or their civilian assistants had carried firearms, and he further claimed that "a lot of people were beaten up, but no one was killed."[108] For his part, Bulandian also stated definitively that "there was no one killed" in the initial attack, but he admitted that during clashes the following night, someone killed a conscript visiting a friend in the dormitory. He hinted that he believed a student was responsible.[109] (While the hardline Iranian press also maintained after the incident that only one person was killed, nearly eleven months later, a Revolutionary Court in Tehran returned [to his family in Shiraz] the body of a long-missing student who had been abducted during the riot; he had been shot in the head.[110])

Bulandian continued to present the regime's spin on events in this interview. He claimed that the Interior Ministry had sought to mollify students by allowing them to stage protests on July 10 and 11, but that "individuals who were not students took undue advantage of those demonstrations, and deviationist slogans were chanted." He further reported that on July 12, Interior Minister Abdulvahid Musavi-Lari had ordered the LEF to tolerate no protests without proper permits. But Bulandian blamed "hooligans and ruffians and elements which did not like the system" for provoking the riots and burning a bus. In response, Bulandian said, the LEF had asked the Basij to help quell the riots.[111]

On July 18, both Khamene'i and Khatami endorsed the formation of a special investigative committee within the powerful Supreme National Security Council (*Shura-yi Amniyat-i Milli*, or SNSC). Chairing this committee was 'Ali Rabi'i—a member of the SNSC secretariat, an advisor to Khatami, and the editor-in-chief of the reformist daily *Kar va Kargar* (Work and Worker). Also serving on the committee were Ibrahim Ra'isi, director of the State Inspectorate-General; Murtaza Riza'i, director of counterintelligence in the IRGC; Ahmad Vahidi, director of intelligence in the IRGC; Abbas 'Ali Farati, prosecutor in Tehran's provincial Military Court; Mustafa Tajzadeh and Ghulamhusayn Bulandian, representatives from the moderately pro-Khatami Ministry of Interior; Ghulamriza Zarifian, representative from the Ministry of Culture and Islamic Guidance; and Jamal Shafi'i, representative from the Ministry of Intelligence and Security.[112] Although the committee could be considered "impartial" in that it was made up of hardliners, moderates, and reformers, the presence of such a broad range of interests allowed each faction to impede inquiry that touched on its respective allies.

Moreover, as the committee deliberated, Iran's power struggle continued unabated. Each broad faction in society encouraged its supporters to maneuver against the other's proxies in the press, Judiciary, and police, even as they presented a united front.[113] Security forces arrested more than 1,500 students during the period of the investigation. Although Khatami claimed that many were released within forty-eight hours, some of those released were quickly rearrested.[114] Six months later, approximately 1,000 students still remained in custody.[115] But the reformists could claim some victories as well. The Investigative Committee detained Dehnamaki and his aide, Suhayl Karimi, at the offices of *Jebheh*, and forced them to testify.[116] Interior Ministry officials subsequently arrested Riza Munjizipur, another *Jebheh* reporter (and, as such, an Ansar-i Hizbullah member).

On August 14, the SNSC released its report. The investigative committee's findings partially excused the violent response to the student protest by citing the number of previous illegal gatherings and marches at the dormitory. Utilizing intelligence from the IRGC as well as reports from the LEF, Interior Ministry, and University Security Department, the report identified fourteen incidents of illegal gatherings and marches at the dormitory between May 1997 and July 1999.[117] The committee criticized government officials for failing to prevent such spontaneous, illegal demonstrations, arguing that tolerance for illegal rallies had caused them to become regular events. Indeed, the report was particularly revealing in its indication of how closely various security and intelligence forces were monitoring students before the riots.

In a clear allusion to Ansar-i Hizbullah and Masud Dehnamaki, the report further confirmed the presence of "certain civilians from the unofficial group" and argued that the presence of "a famous member of a well-known unofficial group in the dormitory area was provocative because the students recognized him." According to the testimony of some LEF personnel, the "people in civilian clothes were encouraging LEF personnel to attack and, using foul language, were reproaching them for not attacking and for not being harsh with the students." As the students retreated into the dormitory, some LEF members testified, LEF officers entered the building "to carry out mopping up operations."[118] In discussing those findings, *Hamshahri* (Fellow Citizen), a popular news and culture newspaper which serves loosely as the Iranian equivalent of *USA Today,* found it significant that, while stopping short of naming the vigilante group, the report at least acknowledged—in the words of *Hamshahri*—the "destructive role of pressure groups."[119]

The SNSC report also shed light on the operations and communications structure of Ansar-i Hizbullah:

> According to the investigations, some of them [the civilians] were informed of the situation by way of a communication system and went to the scene, and a few of them learnt of it through other means and went there. In two cases, the committee investigated the manner of their involvement and could not reach any particular results in preliminary stages. For example, when one of them was asked by the committee: 'How did you learn of the situation?' He answered: 'An anonymous person called me on my mobile telephone and I went there on the basis of the anonymous telephone call.' During preliminary questions, another person gave me the same explanation for the manner of their presence. Another person . . . said he learned of the situation while on patrol on the street.[120]

Notwithstanding an indirect acknowledgment of vigilante involvement in the riots, however, the committee ultimately placed blame on several LEF officials, effectively setting aside the roles played by student provocateurs and vigilantes in the disturbances.[121] Deputy LEF Commander General Mir-Ahmadi, for example, was singled out for aggravating tensions by behaving in a "maladroit manner" upon his arrival after midnight, stirring up trouble with his impromptu inquiry after the protests had already quieted down.

Both hardliners and reformers ultimately expressed dissatisfaction with the SNSC's findings. Reformists were disappointed that the SNSC had entrusted the Intelligence Ministry with the task of investigating the participation of Ansar-i Hizbullah in the rioting. After all, many suspected that the ministry had sympathy for, if not outright links with, Ansar-i Hizbullah and other violent vigilante groups active today. Some Iranian pundits saw the deferral of judgment regarding the responsibility of student groups and hardline vigilantes in the riots as evidence of both the political constraints of justice in the Islamic Republic and the power struggle between the Intelligence and Interior Ministries— in the context of which the latter had not yet acquired the political capital to challenge the former.[122]

Meanwhile, maneuvering between reformists and hardliners continued outside the context of the SNSC report. Even before the outbreak of the rioting, radical hardline judicial chief Ayatollah Muhammad Yazdi was slated to retire. With the accession of his replacement, Ayatollah Mahmud Hashimi-Shahrudi, many in reformist circles hoped that the Judiciary might become less reactionary.[123] Also encouraging to the reformists was the August 25, 1999, dismissal of Brigadier-General Farhad Nazari, chief of the LEF in Tehran (Brigadier-General Muhsin Ansari, deputy to LEF commander Hidayat Lutfian, replaced Nazari).[124]

But Iranian reformists also had good reason to restrain their optimism. In November 1999, a court sentenced Abdullah Nuri, Khatami's minister of the interior and vice president, to five years in prison for allegedly using his newspaper *(Khordad)* insult the Prophet Muhammad and Supreme Leader Khomeini. Khatami refused to intervene to mitigate the sentence.[125] Ansar-i Hizbullah celebrated the verdict, and the hardline daily *Kayhan* lauded an Ansar-i Hizbullah statement warning that reformists would be the first victims of any provocations (presumably, such "provocations" could include any new reform measures).[126] Next, in February 2000, the Judiciary closed down the vast majority of reformist newspapers and journals after reformist candidates won major victories in the first-round 2000 Majlis elections held during the same month. Hamid Najjari, secretary of the hardline *Majma'-i Hizbullah* (Assembly of the Party of God) parliamentary faction, had warned the daily *Azad* before the elections that "even one hair [on the heads] of the members of Ansar-i

Hizbullah is worth more than nationalists, liberals, and pseudo-supporters of the president."[127]

A Trial for the Law Enforcement Forces

As the trial of twenty LEF officers in connection with the dormitory incident opened on February 29, 2000, not one vigilante had yet been charged, while four students had already received death sentences. (On April 30, 2000, Supreme Leader Khamene'i commuted the death sentences to fifteen years of imprisonment.)[128] At the trial, the government prosecutor charged Farhad Nazari (chief of the LEF in Tehran) with ordering the attack, with disobeying the instructions of Interior Minister Abdulvahid Musavi-Lari, and thus with tarnishing the image of the disciplinary forces. Prosecutors charged the other nineteen LEF officers with assault, and one of them faced an additional charge of stealing an electric shaver from the dormitory.[129]

Representing the students was Muhsin Rahami, well known in Iran for his vigorous defense of Khatami ally and former Minister of the Interior Abdullah Nuri. Rahami wasted little time in making his case against both the LEF officials that had been charged and the Ansar-i Hizbullah members, who were never arrested or charged. He accused the security forces of perpetrating attacks—including severe beatings and arson—on Iranians and foreign students.[130] The judge did not give Rahami free rein in court, however, refusing to allow him to question Interior Minister Abdulvahid Musavi-Lari (whose orders Nazari had allegedly contravened) and other high-ranking officials.[131] Rahami later expressed frustration that "the main people involved in the incident are not being tried here."[132]

He proceeded to call a number of witnesses to the stand. Students spoke of being thrown from windows of the dormitory and beaten, their limbs broken in more than a dozen places.[133] Others related that they had suffered fractured skulls; one claimed even to have lost an eye. Still other students complained of stab and slash wounds and of purposeful disfigurement.[134] At the trial's second session, one witness recalled how an assailant in civilian clothes (in other words, not the uniform of the LEF) beat him, forced him into a car, held an empty gun to his head and, pulling the trigger, asked him, "Where is Mr. Khatami to help you now?"[135] Vigilantes beat one of the student witnesses subsequent to his testimony[136] and attacked Muhammad Kazim Kuhi, the dormitory director, one month prior to his own scheduled appearance before the court.[137] Kuhi nevertheless testified, and he laid the blame for the riots squarely on General Mir-Ahmadi, deputy commander of the Tehran Law Enforcement Forces.[138]

Perhaps the most revealing testimony regarding the role of Ansar-i Hizbullah in the attacks was that of student Hasan Rahimi-Nijad, on March 12, 2000, who reported an assault by "assailants who wore white shirts and Colt revolvers and wireless telephones under their clothes."[139] This testimony highlighted both Ansar-i Hizbullah's presence at the dormitory—and the group's noticeable absence before the prosecutor. It further suggested that Ansar-i Hizbullah most likely relies on an informal telephone network to organize itself operationally; the LEF were wearing uniforms and mobilized from barracks and police stations, while the Ansar-i Hizbullah reportedly mobilized by cellular phone. The obvious collaboration between the group and the LEF, as brought out by testimony in the trial, suggests that a high-ranking security official notified one of the Ansar-i Hizbullah leaders, who proceeded to initiate a phone chain, calling adherents of the group to gather at the dormitory.

After the trial, a former Ansar-i Hizbullah activist claimed that, in a previous context, he had once gone to Mashhad with the intent to assassinate 'Abdullah Nuri. The activist revealed that a security officer approached him shortly before Nuri delivered his sermon to say, "The plan has changed. Do not do anything."[140] If true, this separate incident would further illustrate both the extent of coordination among cells of hardliners inside the security apparatuses, and the operational importance of person-to-person telephone contact within Ansar-i Hizbullah.

Farhad Nazari began his defense on March 9, expressing remorse for the students' injuries but denying that the dormitory incident was politically motivated. He instead claimed that the students had threatened and provoked his LEF contingent.[141] Nazari would later argue that student leaders and the reformist press aimed to harm the Islamic Republic by weakening the IRGC, Basij, Intelligence Ministry, and Council of Guardians.[142] Regarding the attack, Nazari contended that he was merely following the orders of his superiors— denying that he had ignored the interior minister's order not to enter the dormitory (presumably indicating either that he did not send his forces into the dormitory, or that the interior minister had not actually given such an order).[143] Deflecting blame away from himself and other LEF officers, Nazari maintained that the reformist press and students like Ahmed Batibi were responsible for tarnishing the image of the security services (Batibi became famous for displaying a bloodied shirt to Western journalists during the riots, an image that the *Economist* would feature on one of its covers).[144] Nazari specifically accused reformist journalists Akbar Ganji and 'Izzatullah Sahabi of spreading lies about the behavior of the security services. (Ganji, a former IRGC official who has become a reformist journalist and who also sat on the [now-banned] reformist daily *Fath*'s editorial board, has become one of the most vocal critics of the Intelligence Ministry. 'Izzatullah Sahabi, son of Iranian Freedom Movement cofounder Yadullah Sahabi, was founding editor of *Iran-i Farda* and remains a prominent reformist.[145])

In later sessions, other defendants took the stand. Colonel Jamshid Khudabakhshi, the former supervisor of an LEF special unit, complained of the "rudeness" of the student rioters and strongly supported Nazari's restraint during the incident. He also claimed that the students had shouted slogans against the police, Ansar-i Hizbullah, and government officials.[146] Farhad Arjumandi, in defending his decision to order the troops under his command to enter the dormitory, condemned the domestic "pen wielders" (the reformist press) who had poisoned the atmosphere in Iran, encouraging the disrespect among students toward regime hardliners in general, and toward the LEF and other security forces in particular.[147] Finally, on May 28, 2000, the trial ended with Nazari declaring, "As an expert, I say that I know of no country in the world that condemns its police for taking action against obvious crimes."[148]

On July 11, 2000, Judge Ahmad Tabataba'i found the LEF defendants innocent of almost all charges.[149] Only LEF members Badrazadeh and Arjumandi were found guilty, the former on the charge of stealing an electric shaver, the latter for assault. But beyond the incredulity Iranian reformists shared upon hearing the "not guilty" verdicts was a greater concern about the absence of accountability for the numerous Ansar-i Hizbullah vigilantes who had participated in the attack, as well as the absence of a sufficient explanation as to how the group came to coordinate its actions with the official security forces.

The Persistent Hardline Threat to Reform

When Iran's hardline Press Court closed the majority of the country's reformist papers in February 2000, the weekly *Litharat al-Husayn* published an Ansar-i Hizbullah statement declaring, "The forces of Hizbullah nationwide have been put on a state of alert to put down the outlaws and agitators."[150] Such a declaration again raised the possibility that the LEF and the vigilante group might have been acting in unison, in that Ansar-i Hizbullah was publicly declaring its intention to work inside the LEF's domain while apparently neither antagonizing nor eliciting a response from the security forces. Less than four months after the riots, hardline cleric Hojjatolislam Parvazi issued a pamphlet warning Khatami that, despite his electoral mandate, "things" were happening in Qum and Tehran, and that the "Sons of War" would pose a threat, presumably to reform in general, if not to Khatami himself in particular.[151] He referred to the expansion of Ansar-i Hizbullah and warned that the group was growing more ambitious in its selection of targets. Parvazi also related a conversation he had with Ansar-i Hizbullah activists in which they argued that, in their view, "the key to the Revolution's survival is the spread of terror and intimidation among the people."[152]

The following month, approximately fifty vigilantes attacked the popular Andisheh Cultural Complex, assaulting the director. Operated by the reformist-leaning Ministry of Culture and Islamic Guidance, the complex was a natural target for a group whose newspaper repeatedly condemned the minister of culture. According to one employee, the assailants declared, "We will do to you what we did to the students in the university dorms. Leave this place quickly."[153]

In a move exhibiting his contempt for the students, Khamene'i removed Brigadier-General Hidayat Lutfian from the directorship of the LEF on June 28, 2000, and reappointed him to a high-level position in the armed forces general staff the very next day.[154] Authorities arrested Muhsin Rahami, the students' lawyer, the day of Lutfian's reappointment, and the Tehran Judiciary released a statement explaining that Rahami had been "detained on charges of disturbing public opinion in connection with taped remarks against some officials of the Islamic Republic of Iran."[155] On July 6, the Judiciary issued a statement declaring that Rahami and his colleague Shirin Ibadi would be tried behind closed doors.[156]

Meanwhile, the influential reformist-leaning student group known as the Office for Fostering Unity (OFU) accused the Judiciary of again moving to crack down on students. In June 2000, security forces arrested several student leaders and released them only after they agreed to sign pledges that they would no longer participate in rallies or demonstrations. Akbar Atri, a member of OFU's board of trustees and himself charged with "spreading lies and disturbing public opinion," stated on June 10, "After closing down almost all pro-reform newspapers, the Judiciary has now concentrated on student groups in its crackdown on the popular reform program."[157]

But the Judiciary was particularly annoyed with Rahami's alleged role in distributing the videotaped confession of self-described Ansar-i Hizbullah official Amir Farshad Ibrahimi. Ironically, by arresting Rahami, the government gave greater credibility to the videotape. As Rahami remained in jail (he was freed on bail only on July 22, 2000), several hundred Ansar-i Hizbullah members once again violently attacked a group of students who were peacefully protesting the one-year anniversary of the dormitory attack.[158] And when Supreme Leader Khamene'i intervened in the first debate of the new Majlis (which took place in August 2000) in order to prohibit a legislative attempt to liberalize the press law, Ansar-i Hizbullah called for the death of lawmakers who objected to the law's suppression.[159]

Conclusions

In the wake of the July 1999 riots, Ansar-i Hizbullah has become more than a nuisance. In fact, the group's activities could provide a significant pretext for a hardline crackdown on reform by hardliners. During the 1999 rioting, twenty-four senior IRGC commanders (including four implicated by Sa'id Imami in the 1998 dissident murders described in Chapter 4) sent Khatami a letter declaring, "If you do not make a revolutionary decision [to suppress the students, one of Khatami's chief power bases] and if you do not fulfill your Islamic national mission today, tomorrow will be far too late. . . . We cannot tolerate this situation any longer if it is not dealt with."[160] When the riots were quieted, the threat made by the IRGC commanders faded into the background, although in April 2000, rumors of an impending coup again circulated in Tehran as an IRGC statement declared, "When the time comes, small and big enemies will feel the revolutionary hammer on their skulls."[161] Given Ansar-i Hizbullah's continued hostility toward Khatami, the IRGC statements raise the possibility that vigilantes could provoke a crisis that would provide security forces with the excuse to clamp down on reformists or—if the crisis were severe enough—to unseat the president himself.

Yet, the fact that Ansar-i Hizbullah continues to operate indicates that the Iranian government, despite the reformist rhetoric of President Khatami, remains either unable or unwilling to crack down on the hardline vigilantes. Even if the statements of self-described Ansar-i Hizbullah defectors are not completely accurate, circumstantial evidence does suggest that Ansar-i Hizbullah receives official protection at the highest levels. For example:

- Ansar-i Hizbullah vigilantes have seldom been charged and have never served time in prison for even their most violent attacks, including their July 1999 assault on the Tehran University dormitory.
- The raid on the dormitory indicates a high level of intelligence sharing, if not outright coordination, between the group and Iran's official security services.
- Ansar-i Hizbullah is sufficiently well financed to maintain a full-fledged weekly newspaper, although it refuses to disclose its source of funding.
- Ansar-i Hizbullah has access to hardware that, by law, is restricted to Iran's official security services.
- Ayatollah Ahmad Jannati and other high-level officials repeatedly make statements that support Ansar-i Hizbullah's goals, and they have so far refused to publicly condemn the group's methods.

While groups like Ansar-i Hizbullah continue to spew anti-Western rhetoric, their chief targets remain in the domestic sphere. Indeed, the near-constant intimidation posed by these groups stymies reform in Iran and creates the potential for violence in the form of an even more significant hardline crackdown in the future.

Notes

1. Said Amir Arjomand, *The Turban for the Crown: The Islamic Revolution in Iran* (New York: Oxford University Press, 1988), p. 173.
2. Kenneth Katzman, *The Warriors of Islam: Iran's Revolutionary Guard* (Boulder, Colorado: Westview Press, 1993), p. 84.
3. "An interview with Dr. Ali Abbaspour," *Shuma*, March 5, 1998, online at www.netiran.com/Htdocs/Clippings/DPolitics/980305XXDP03.html
4. Most recently, several formal political groups have taken the name "hizbullah" and, as official parliamentary and political factions, do

not belong to the "vigilante group" classification. Following the 1996 inauguration of the Fifth Majlis, for example, two such groups formed. One was called the Party of God Assembly *(Majma'-i Hizbullah)*, comprising representatives from the leftist faction and Servants of Reconstruction (a pro-Rafsanjani faction). The other group, called the Party of God Faction *(Fraksiun-i Hizbullah)*, comprised representatives from the *Jama'a-yi Ruhaniyyat-i Mubariz* (the majority in the Fourth Majlis). A third party, the *Mustaqillin-i Hizbullah*, exists as an independent group, but its power was greatly diminished in the last (February 2000) elections.

5. *Manatiq-i Azad,* June 28, 1999, in Iran News Press Roundup, provided by Gulf 2000 Project website, online at http://gulf2000.columbia.edu

6. Michael Theodoulou, "Iran Zealot Polices Hemlines," *The Times* (London), August 18, 1999.

7. Michael Theodoulou, "One Man's Mission: Staying True to Khomeini" *Christian Science Monitor,* September 13, 1999.

8. *Risalat,* October 23, 1995; "Guards Corps 'Reviewing the File' on Head of Ansar-e Hezbollah Group," Islamic Republic News Agency (IRNA), April 14, 1998.

9. Ibrahimi also claims that Allah-Karam co-owned a computer company on Mirdamad Road in Tehran, as well as a computer importing firm on Zardasht Road. See "Hizbullah Member Reveals Plots Against Reformists," *ash-Sharq al-Awsat,* June 4, 2000, p. 6, in FBIS (GMP20000605000115/140).

10. Muhammad Quchani, "Children of Rage," *Asr-i Azadagan,* April 8, 2000, p. 3, in FBIS (IAP20000419000019).

11. "Hizbullah Member Reveals Plots Against Reformists."

12. Ibid.

13. Masud Kuhistani Nijad, "Introducing the Islamic Mo'talefeh [Coalition] Association [An interview with Mr. Habibollah Asgar Owladi]," *Guzaresh,* no. 93, October 1998, online at www.netiran.com/Htdocs/Clippings/DPolitics/981022XXDP01.htm

14. *Al-Mujaz'an Iran,* no. 87, December 1998, p. 18.

15. *Kayhan,* August 27, 1995, as quoted in *Iran Brief,* June 3, 1996.

16. "Hezbollah's Presence Safeguards Islamic Values," *Tehran Times* (internet edition), December 23, 1995, online at www.tehrantimes.com

17. See, for example, Alex Efty, "Khamenei Calls for 'Perpetual Struggle' against U.S.," Agence France Presse, November 2, 1989.

18. "American Elections Zionist Managed, Says Iranian Ayatollah," IRNA, November 14, 1992, reprinted in *Moneyclips*, November 14, 1992.

19. "Hardliner: All Americans Traveling to Iran Are Suspicious," Associated Press Worldstream, December 4, 1998.

20. "Hizbullah Member Reveals Plots against Reformists."

21. Ibid.

22. Speech by Parvazi, as reproduced in 'Ali Riza Nurizadeh, *Guzarish-i Qatliha va Iarafat-i Sa'id Imami* (Report on the murders and confessions of Sa'id Imami) (Spanga, Sweden: Baran, 1999), p. 19.

23. "Hizbullah Member Reveals Plots against Reformists."

24. Ibid.

25. Speech by Parvazi, as reproduced in Nurizadeh, p. 19.

26. Abbas Samii, "Profile of an Iranian Journalist," Radio Free Europe/ Radio Liberty (RFE/RL) *Iran Report* 1, no. 4, December 21, 1998.

27. Michael Eisenstadt, *Iranian Military Power: Capabilities and Intentions* (Washington, DC: The Washington Institute for Near East Policy, 1996), p. 71.

28. Wilfried Buchta, *Who Rules Iran? The Structure of Power in the Islamic Republic* (Washington, DC: The Washington Institute for Near East Policy and Konrad Adenauer Stiftung, 2000), p. 74.

29. Samii, "Profile of an Iranian Journalist."

30. Quchani, p. 3.

31. Hujjat Murtaji, *Jinahha-yi siyasi dar Iran imruz* (Political factions in contemporary Iran) (Tehran: Intisharat-i Naqsh va Nigar, 1998), p. 93.

32. Ibid.

33. Quchani, p. 3.

34. Ibid.

35. Interview by author with an Iranian regional interest group member, November 1999.

36. Ibid.

37. Interviews by author in Iran, August 1999.

38. Ibid.

39. Interviews by author in Isfahan, June 1996 and July 1999.

40. Quchani, p. 3.

41. Abbas Samii, "Publications Come and Go," RFE/RL *Iran Report* 2, no. 6, February 8, 1999.

42. Murtaji, p. 93.

43. "Pressure Groups and the National Media," *Bahar*, July 23, 2000, pp. 1, 16.

44. *Iran News*, February 28, 1999, provided by Gulf 2000 Project website, online at http://gulf2000.columbia.edu; "Majlis Deputy Sued after Calling Daily 'Subversive'," *Neshat* (internet edition), May 31, 1999, in BBC Worldwide Monitoring.

45. "Two More Iranian Reporters Arrested," Deutsche Presse Agentur, August 1, 1999.

46. Muhammad 'Ali Zikriyayi, *Hijdahum Tir Mah '78* (Tehran: Intisharat-i Kuyar, 1999), p. 404.

47. Murtaji, p. 93; "An Interview with Dr. Ali Abbaspour," *Shuma*, March 5, 1998; Quchani, p. 3.

48. "Jebheh Weekly Banned," IRNA, April 29, 2000.

49. *Iran News*, February 28, 1999.

50. "The Sound of the Dead: A Chat with Managing Directors of Banned Journals," *Payam-i Imruz*, no. 39, June 2000, online at www.netiran.com/Htdocs/WeeklyJournal/Politics/wj00205.htm

51. "Hardline Iranian Weekly to Appeal against Ban," Reuters, January 5, 1999.

52. Reuters, August 18, 1997.

53. David Hirst, "Iranian Clerics' Power Struggle Getting Personal," *St. Petersburg Times*, January 23, 1998, p. A16 (reprinted in greater detail from *The Guardian*, January 17, 1998).

54. "Iranian President Adopts More Hostile Tone against the United States," Agence France Presse, January 19, 1998.

55. "Iran Paper Promises Prize for Killing of Dissident," Reuters, September 11, 1999.

56. Theodoulou, "One Man's Mission: Staying True to Khomeini."

57. "Ansar-i Hizbullah Needs a Third Camp?" *Nim-Niga*, October 5, 1999, p. 14.

58. "Iranian Threats to 'Satanic Verses' Editor Raises Concern," Agence France Presse, June 3, 2000.

59. "Ansar-i Hizbullah Needs a Third Camp?"

60. "The Sound of the Dead: A Chat with Managing Directors of Banned Journals."

61. Speech by Parvazi, as reproduced in Nurizadeh, p. 16.

62. *Haftehnameh-yi Siyasat*, no. 6, 28/5/1377, as quoted in Murtaji, p. 93.

63. Quchani, p. 3.

64. Speech by Parvazi, as reproduced in Nurizadeh, pp. 16–17.

65. Quchani, p. 3; speech by Parvazi, as reproduced in Nurizadeh, pp. 16–17.

66. "Miserable Plight of a Brilliant Scholar," *Muslim News*, May 31, 1996.

67. "Funeral Service Reportedly Ends in Confrontation," *Kayhan*, July 20, 1995, p. 1, in FBIS-NES-95-174, September 8, 1995, p. 79.

68. Mehrdad Balali, "Hezbollahis Step up Pressure as Cultures Clash in Tehran," Agence France Presse, October 24, 1995.

69. "Iranian Philosopher's Speech at Tehran University Disrupted," Voice of Israel external service, October 12, 1995, in BBC Summary of World Broadcasts, October 14, 1995 (EE/D2434/ME).

70. "Daily Addresses 'Incident' at Tehran University," *Salam*, October 14, 1995, p. 2, in FBIS-NES-95-205, October 24, 1995, p. 66.

71. "Daily Explains 'Incidents' at Tehran University," *Salam*, October 16, 1995, p. 3, in FBIS-NES-95-206, October 25, 1996, p. 74.

72. "Ansar-e Hezbollah, Khamene'i's Helpers," *Iran Brief*, June 3, 1996.

73. "Hezbollah Gang Threatens to Hang Deviant University Students," *Salam*, May 9, 1996, in BBC Summary of World Broadcasts, May 14, 1996 (EE/D2612/ME).

74. "Ansar-e Hezbollah Strike Again," *Seraj*, November 15, 1997, online at www.seraj.org/news.htm

75. "Vigilantes Assault People after Lecture by Controversial Thinker," Associated Press, January 15, 2000; "News Update on Dr. Soroush," July 1, 2000, www.seraj.org/news.htm

76. BBC Worldwide Monitoring, June 20, 2000.

77. Deutsche Presse Agentur, August 27, 2000.

78. "Militants in Iran Renew Their Attacks on Western Influences," *New York Times*, May 9, 1996.

79. "Radical Elements Raided Movie Theatre in Tehran, Beat up Audience," Deutsche Presse Agentur, May 6, 1996.

80. Nurizadeh, p. 25; "Hizbullah Member Reveals Plots against Reformists."

81. "Hizbullah Member Reveals Plots against Reformists."

82. "Iran: Hezbollah Threatens to Close Majles, Blacklists New Members," *ash-Sharq al-Awsat*, June 4, 1996, pp. 1, 4, in FBIS-NES-96-108.

83. William Drozdiak, "German Court: Tehran Ordered Exile Killings," *Washington Post*, April 11, 1997, p. 1.

84. "Islamic Hardliner Threatens Suicide Attack on Embassy," Agence France Presse, April 11, 1997.

85. "Iran: Students Clash with Police at German Embassy Protest," Agence France Presse, April 14, 1997.

86. "Police Ease Security around German Embassy," Agence France Presse, April 19, 1997.

87. "Fundamentalists Beat up Liberal Newspaper Editor in Iran," Agence France Presse, August 1, 1998.

88. "Political Group Says It Was Not Involved in Attack against Officials," IRNA, September 5, 1998.

89. "Khatami Dismissed Najafabadi from Security Ministry," *ash-Sharq al-Awsat*, January 8, 1999, in FBIS-NES-99-008.

90. *Subh-i Imruz*, November 10, 1999, in Iran News Press Review, provided by Gulf 2000 Project website, online at http://gulf2000.columbia.edu

91. "Iran's New Leadership Curbs Power of Morality Enforcers," *The Plain Dealer* (Cleveland), April 25, 1998.

92. "Guards Corps 'Reviewing the File' on Head of the Ansar-e Hezbollah Group," IRNA, April 16, 1998.

93. Nurizadeh, p. 25.

94. "Amir Kabir University Reacts to 'Recent Incident'," *Salam*, October 16, 1995, p. 2, in FBIS-NES-95-210, October 31, 1996, p. 89.

95. Speech by Parvazi, as reproduced in Nurizadeh, p. 15.

96. Elaine Sciolino, "Iran Protests Spread to 18 Cities; Police Crack Down at University," *New York Times*, July 13, 1999, p. A1.

97. Interview by author in Tehran, July 1999.

98. "Several Injured in Clash between Students and Security Forces," IRNA, July 9, 1999, in BBC Worldwide Monitoring, July 9, 1999.

99. Geneive Abdo, "Iran on Brink as Students Riot," *The Observer*, July 11, 1999, p. 22.

100. Sciolino, "Iran Protests Spread to 18 Cities."

101. Douglas Jehl, "Despite Police Dismissals, Iran Protest Is the Angriest Yet," *New York Times*, July 12, 1999, p. A4.

102. Author observation, Tehran, July 1999.

103. *Hamshahri*, August 11, 1999. Translation provided by Student Movement Coordinating Committee for Democracy in Iran (SMCCDI), a Dallas-based organization espousing a reformist position often critical of the regime. SMCCDI's daily press translations offer access to a wide variety of Iranian newspapers and, more importantly, remain unadulterated.

104. Interview with Masud Dehnamaki, *Tavanah,* no. 46, Murdad 4, 1378 [July 1953], p. 14, as reproduced in Zikriyayi, *Hijdahum Tir Mah '78,* p. 338.

105. Jehl, "Despite Police Dismissals, Iran Protest Is the Angriest Yet."

106. Author observation, Tehran, July 1999.

107. Author interviews in Tehran, July 1999.

108. "Security Officials Describe Unrest Incidents at Tehran University," Vision of the Islamic Republic of Iran Network 1, July 17, 1999, in BBC Worldwide Monitoring, through Global NewsBank, online at www.newsbank.com

109. Ibid.

110. Reuters, May 24, 2000.

111. Ibid.

112. "Supreme National Security Council's Findings on Dormitory Attack," Vision of the Islamic Republic of Iran Network 1, August 14, 1999, in BBC Worldwide Monitoring, August 16, 1999.

113. Interview by author with an Islamic Republic government official, Tehran, August 1999.

114. "More Student Unrest Leaders Detained in Tehran," Deutsche Presse Agentur, August 8, 1999; "Partial Listing of the Arrested Students and Their Illegal Status," SMCCDI News Service, January 3, 2000; *Subh-i Imruz,* January 10, 2000, provided by SMCDDI, www.daneshjoo.org

115. "Tehran Police Face Court Martial Next Week over Bloody Unrest," Agence France Presse, February 23, 2000.

116. "Two Radical Islamists Leaders Arrested in Tehran," Deutsche Presse Agentur, July 29, 1999; *Subh-i Imruz,* July 31, 1999, provided by SMCDDI, www.daneshjoo.org

117. For information on the coordination of intelligence services in Iran, see Nurizadeh, pp. 100–101; "Supreme National Security Council's Findings on Dormitory Attack."

118. "Supreme National Security Council's Findings on Dormitory Attack."

119. "Student Movement Acquitted," *Hamshahri,* August 16, 1999, p. 1, in FBIS-NES-1999-1118.

120. "Supreme National Security Council's Findings on Dormitory Attack."

121. Ibid.

122. "Majlis Deputies Say Report on Tehran Riots 'Not Complete'," *Iran News* (internet edition), August 16, 1999, in BBC Worldwide Monitoring, through Global NewsBank, August 16, 1999, online at www.newsbank.com

123. "New Head of Judiciary 'Will Not Enter into Any Political Factionalism'," IRNA, August 17, 1999.

124. "Iran Fires Tehran Police Chief Implicated in July Hostel Raid," Associated Press Worldstream, August 25, 1999.

125. "Reformers Condemn and Hardliners Welcome Jailing of Nuri," Agence France Presse, November 30, 1999; "President Khatami Says He Will Not Intervene for Abdollah Nouri," November 28, 1999. For the transcript of the trial, see *Shawkaran-i Islah* [Hemlock for a reformer] (Tehran: Intisharat-i Tarh-i Naw, 1999).

126. "Abdullah Nuri's Explanations in Court Have Convinced the Public of His Guilt," *Kayhan*, November 29, 1999, online at www.kayhannews.com

127. "Iran News Election Reports," *Iran News*, December 26, 1999, provided by Gulf 2000 Project website, online at http://gulf2000.columbia.edu

128. "Iran Says It Spares Four Students from Hanging after July Unrest," Agence France Presse, April 30, 2000, "Real Culprits Not on Trial, Iran Police Court Martial Told," Agence France Presse, March 4, 2000.

129. "First Hearing in Trial of Dormitory Incident Held," *Tehran Times*, March 1, 2000, online at www. terhrantimes.com; "July Unrest Police Trial, First Session," IranMania, www.iranmania.com/news/policetrial/session1.asp

130. "July Unrest Police Trial, First Session."

131. "July Unrest Police Trial, Fifth Session," IranMania, www.iranmania.com/news/policetrial/session5.asp

132. "In Tehran Trial, Students Recount Police Brutality," Associated Press, March 4, 2000.

133. Afshin Valinejad, "Iran Students Narrate Beatings," Associated Press, February 29, 2000.

134. "July Unrest Police Trial, First Session."

135. "July Unrest Police Trial, Second Session," IranMania, www.iranmania.com/news/policetrial/session2.asp

136. "Real Culprits Not on Trial, Iran Police Court Martial Told."

137. "Countdown to Final Ballot," *Iran News* (internet edition), February 13, 2000.

138. "July Unrest Police Trial, Third Session," IranMania, www.iranmania.com/news/policetrial/session3.asp

139. "Complainants Take the Stand in Fifth Hearing of Dormitory Incident," IRNA, March 12, 2000.

140. "Hizbullah Member Reveals Plots against Reformists," *ash-Sharq al-Awsat*, June 4, 2000, p. 6.

141. "July Unrest Police Trial, Fourth Session," IranMania, www.iranmania.com/news/policetrial/session4.asp

142. "Ousted Tehran Police Chief in Court again over Deadly Student Unrest," Agence France Presse, May 8, 2000; "July Unrest Police Trial, Tenth Session," IranMania, www.iranmania.com/news/policetrial/session10.asp

143. "Ousted Tehran Police Chief Says Police Acted within the Law," Agence France Presse, April 29, 2000.

144. "July Unrest Police Trial, Twelfth Session," IranMania, www.iranmania.com/news/policetrial/session12.asp

145. Buchta, p. 83.

146. "July Unrest Police Trial, Eleventh Session," IranMania, www.iranmania.com/news/policetrial/session11.asp

147. "Eleventh Court Hearing for Former Police Chief Held," IRNA, May 13, 2000.

148. "July Unrest Police Trial, Fifteenth Session," IranMania, www.iranmania.com/news/policetrial/session15.asp

149. Ali Raiss-Tousi, "Tehran Police Acquitted of Hostel Assault," Reuters, July 11, 2000.

150. "Islamic Militia 'on Alert' to Deal with Social Unrest," Agence France Presse, April 29, 2000.

151. Speech by Parvazi, as reproduced in Nurizadeh, p. 16; "A Report on the Case of the Serial Killings after One Year"; *Payam-i Imru*, no. 34, November 1999, provided by Iran News.

152. "A Report on the Case of the Serial Killings after One Year."

153. "Popular Cultural Center Attacked by 'Commandos,' Agence France Presse, May 23, 2000.

154. "Former Police Chief Gets Top Military Post," Agence France Presse, June 29, 2000.

155. "Rahami, Ebadi Receive Arrest Warrants," IRNA, June 28, 2000.

156. "Iran Lawyers to Be Tried behind Closed Doors," Reuters, July 6, 2000.

157. Ali Akbar Dareini, "Iranian Hardliners Cracking Down on Student Activists," Associated Press, June 10, 2000.

158. 'Ali Raiss-Tousi, "Islamic Vigilantes Take Control of Tehran Square," Reuters, July 8, 2000.

159. "Leaders Decree Receives Nationwide Support," *Tehran Times* (internet edition), August 8, 2000, online at www.tehrantimes.com; "Iranian Hardliners Protest Reformist Lawmaker," August 8, 2000, www.cnn.com

160. "Suspicions Grow Iran Hardliners are Trying to Unseat Khatami," *al-Watan*, July 21, 1999, in *Mideast Mirror*, July 21, 1999; "Military Commanders Give an Ultimatum to President Khatami," *Jumhuri-yi Islami*, July 19, 1999, in BBC Worldwide Monitoring, July 19, 1999.

161. Guy Dinmore, "Reformists Accuse Iran's Hardliners of Plotting Coup," *Financial Times*, April 20, 2000, p. 5.

Chapter 4

The Widening Web: Intelligence Ministry Complicity in Vigilantism

If vigilantism in Iran were linked only to the core group of Ansar-i Hizbullah followers, then the threat that pressure groups pose might be more easily maintained. Ansar-i Hizbullah, while helping to provoke the worst rioting in Iran since the 1979 Islamic Revolution, limited its attacks to Iranian intellectuals and, with the exception of the attack on the Amirabad dormitory, often carried out its attacks with minimal loss of life. But a newly reincarnated, Khatami-era Fida'iyan-i Islam, described below, enlarged the dimensions of the vigilante threat, linking the Iranian government more closely to the hardline pressure groups and raising further questions about the extent to which Iranian officials themselves are complicit in supporting the vigilantes.

Fida'iyan-i Islam's Khatami-Era Incarnation

During the final years of Ayatollah Khomeini's life and the first years of 'Ali Khamene'i's reign as Supreme Leader beginning in 1989, Fida'iyan-i Islam remained quietly supportive of the government. But the increasing social and political discord accompanying Muhammad Khatami's rise to power in the late 1990s again gave rise to Fida'iyan-i Islam activity. This time, anti-Americanism provided a focus for the organization.

Following Khatami's call for a "dialogue of civilizations" first expressed during a Cable News Network interview in January 1998, a number of Americans sought to meet their former adversaries; two of the most prominent were former U.S. embassy hostages Barry Rosen (the embassy press attaché at the time of the crisis) and Bruce Laingen (the former chargé d'affaires). On November 9, 1998, the Iranian hardline daily *Quds* published a threat from someone who called the newspaper claiming to be affiliated with the Fida'iyan-i Islam. The group reportedly "warned that it considers itself duty bound to carry out suicide attacks against Bruce Laingen and Barry Rosen and other individuals associated with the den of spies if they return to Iran."[1] Rosen and Laingen, in the end, cancelled their planned visit.

Two weeks after this threat was issued, a busload of visiting American businessmen approaching their hotel in fashionable northern Tehran were attacked. Vigilantes stopped the minibus and proceeded to break all the windows; flying glass injured several of the Americans. The Fida'iyan-i Islam claimed responsibility for this action, both in the London-based Arabic daily *al-Hayat* and in a statement released in Tehran. *Al-Hayat* reported having received a warning from an anonymous caller shortly after the attack, who cautioned, "What happened is a lesson and a warning to all spies."[2]

This incident can best be seen in the context of the power struggle between the hardliners and the more moderate Khatami faction. Indeed, in its claim of responsibility for the bus attack, the Fida'iyan-i Islam declared it to be "an operation against U.S. spies and a warning to the officials who invited them."[3] IRNA reported that demonstrators at a subsequent (November 27) rally organized by Ansar-i Hizbullah in support of the attack—hundreds of hardliners demonstrated in Tehran and two provincial cities despite an official ban— warned against any further attempt to invite Americans to visit Iran, stating that such an attempt "will be confronted more severely."[4] Indeed, the following summer, a group of American graduate students sponsored by the American Institute of Iranian Studies departed Iran suddenly at the U.S. State Department's request, presumably after the U.S. government received word of a threat or impending attack against them.[5] The "involvement" after the attack by Ansar-i Hizbullah in the form of the hardline rally raises the question of whether that group and Fida'iyan-i Islam might be fronts for the same organization or, what is more likely, whether the two groups have common ties or share some membership or patronage overlap. But a subsequent series of attacks on Iranian writers and intellectuals raises the larger question of whether Fida'iyan-i Islam might be acting for another organization much more closely linked to the hardline Iranian Intelligence Ministry.

The Dissident Murders

The new incarnation of Fida'iyan-i Islam did not limit its threats—and may not have limited its attacks—to Americans. On November 22, 1998, the bodies of Darius Foruhar and his wife, Parvaneh Iskandari, were found in their Tehran home. This double murder was particularly brutal: Darius had been stabbed twenty-six times, his wife twenty-five.[6] When IRNA briefly mentioned the murders at the conclusion of the evening newscast, the population was shocked.[7] Foruhar was neither a marginal dissident nor an obscure writer known only to the elite; rather, he had been a political and cultural figure in Iran for more than half a century. Meanwhile, former Revolutionary Guard commander Muhsin Riza'i blamed the crime on "pressure groups linked to the Zionists."[8]

Darius Foruhar had first risen to prominence in 1944 when, at the age of fifteen, he began organizing pro–Muhammad Musaddiq demonstrations. As a student at the University of Tehran, Foruhar co-founded the nationalist Pan-Iranist Party. Feeling that his colleague Muhsin Piziskhpur was insufficiently pro-Musaddiq, however, Foruhar eventually quit the party. In 1951, he founded his own ultranationalist party, the *Hizb-i Pan-Iranist-i Iran* (Pan-Iranist Party of Iran), which called for the reintegration of Bahrain, Afghanistan, and the Caucasus into Iran. It was vehemently anti-clerical, anti-royalist, anti-Semitic, anti-Arab, and anti-Turk.[9] Over time Foruhar grew more moderate, although he continued to oppose the shah. In May 1977, in the boldest act of open criticism since Khomeini's 1963 speeches, fifty-three lawyers sent an open letter to the shah accusing him of interfering in the Judiciary; Foruhar was among the prominent nationalists who subsequently went further, accusing the shah of despotism in another open letter.[10] Observing that the shah and the SAVAK intelligence and security organization allowed this kind vocal criticism, Foruhar, along with his two colleagues in his dispatch to the shah, revived the old pro-Musaddiq National Front under the name "Union of National Front Forces."[11] With the 1979 establishment of the Islamic Republic, Foruhar became the labor minister under the short-lived provisional government of Prime Minister Mehdi Bazargan. Afterward, Foruhar remained active as a voice of intellectual dissent, even while quietly living in effective retirement until his untimely death.

But the murder of the Foruhars was only the beginning of a string of dissident attacks. Three days after the couple's bodies were discovered, that of Majid Sharif, a reformist writer and translator, was found among unidentified bodies in the Tehran coroner's office. Sharif had been missing for almost a week and reportedly died of a heart attack, although some suspect that the heart attack was induced by a potassium injection.[12] Shortly thereafter, Muhammad Mukhtari, a dissident poet, was strangled after shopping in northern Tehran's fashionable Tajrish Square. On December 9, 1998, Mukhtari's body was found in Shahr-i Rayy, on the southern edge of Tehran. That same day, another reformist writer, Muhammad Jafar Puyandeh, disappeared; his body was discovered three days later.[13]

On December 21, the pro-Khatami reformist newspaper *Khurdad* published Fida'iyan-i Islam's claim of responsibility for the killings: "The revolutionary execution of Darius Foruhar, Parvaneh Iskandari, Muhammad Mukhtari, and Muhammad Jafar Puyandeh is a warning to all mercenary writers and their counter-value supporters who are cherishing the idea of spreading corruption and promiscuity in the country and bringing back foreign domination over Iran."[14]

Some reformist newspapers claimed that the real death toll from the string of Iranian dissident murders extended back to October 1994, when 134 writers signed an open letter protesting the government's "censorship and harassment" and "anti-democratic practices."[15] Soon afterward, five of the signatories were killed or died under mysterious circumstances.[16] Then, in August 1996, some reformist writers en route to a conference in Armenia at the invitation of Iran's Ministry of Culture and Islamic Guidance narrowly avoided being killed in a suspicious crash. Reportedly, the bus driver, Khusru Barati, jumped out of the bus after directing it toward a cliff.[17] One of the passengers grabbed the wheel and brought the bus under control.[18]

Regardless of when they began, however, the so-called "serial killings" of dissidents caused widespread outrage in Iran. Reformist-leaning President Khatami, although silent in the face of other human rights abuses, strongly condemned the murders. Blame flew inside the Iranian power structure. Mirroring the widening schism within the Iranian government between reformists and hardliners, the hardline Judiciary issued a statement labeling the murders a "mysterious and organized move inspired by foreign elements," while hardline Intelligence Minister Qurban 'Ali Durri-Najafabadi blamed "American and Israeli spies."[19] Meanwhile, Iranian reformists openly speculated about the involvement of the Intelligence Ministry in the murders,[20] and Khatami's allies sensed a plot. Mustafa Tajzadeh, deputy minister of the moderately pro-Khatami Ministry of Interior, speculated on the motives of the attackers in reformist *Zan*: "Anarchy will make society thirsty for security, and people will pay any price to get that security, even if they lose their legitimate rights and freedom."[21]

In 1999, Khatami formed a three-member committee to investigate the killings. He kept the members' names secret for security reasons, although they were later leaked: Hojjatolislam 'Ali Yunisi, head of the Judicial Organization of the Armed Forces and widely seen as closer to Khamene'i than to Khatami; 'Ali Rabi'i, an advisor to Khatami and editor-in-chief of the reformist daily *Kar va Kargar*; and 'Ali Sarmadi, a deputy intelligence minister (the Intelligence Ministry has traditionally been much more deferential to the hardline Khamene'i than to Khatami). Rabi'i had previously served a stint as deputy under Minister of Intelligence 'Ali Fallahian and, in July and August 1999, had chaired the special Supreme National Security Council committee investigating the July 1999 attack on the Tehran University dormitory.[22]

Suspicion during the investigation quickly fell on the Intelligence Ministry. 'Ali Rabi'i spoke with several friends of Darius Foruhar, who told him that Foruhar knew the security services had bugged his home and telephone. When Rabi'i then went to the Intelligence Ministry to ask for the tape of Foruhar's last phone call, he was told that the tape had been erased.[23]

From this point, the murder investigation quickly escalated into a high-level power struggle. On January 6, 1999, the Intelligence Ministry admitted its own complicity, stating, "A few of our colleagues—irresponsible, devious, and obstinate persons—were among those arrested [for the murders]."[24] The London-based pan-Arabic *ash-Sharq al-Awsat* reported the following day that Intelligence Minister Durri-Najafabadi had submitted his resignation to President Khatami, although the president did not immediately accept it. More ominously, the unattributed article reported that Ayatollah Ahmad Jannati, the powerful hardline cleric linked to Ansar-i Hizbullah, had meanwhile called for Khatami's ouster, having become upset with continuing reformist trends and investigation of hardline security officers.[25] The administration went on to arrest ten suspects from the intelligence community in late January and four more the following month; one suspect was detained by Turkish police and returned to Iran.[26] Iran's Judiciary later referred to the involvement of a total twenty-seven "rogue" intelligence agents.[27] Yet, even as authorities rounded up suspects in the killings, the Fida'iyan-i Islam issued a new statement, declaring:

> We should announce that the Pure Muhammadan Devotees of Mustafa Navvab [Fida'iyan-i Islam] have a well-organized structure, following certain regulations in their missions. This group, through relentless efforts, has

opened a file for each and every sold-out and hypocritical person using the culture and thought as a safe haven to launch their endless attacks on the principles of the system. In its recent operation, the judicial unit of the group, consisting of three experienced and fair judges, tried in absentia and condemned to death this group of people. . . . We believe that had these trials taken place in normal courts of law free from any political pressures, the results would have been the same and we only accelerated the procedure.[28]

On February 9, 1999, Khatami finally accepted Durri-Najafabadi's resignation,[29] yet Durri-Najafabadi was defiant to the end. He complained bitterly of his disgrace and of the ingratitude of the Iranian people, lambasting unnamed enemies "from outside and inside the country" for his downfall and for tarnishing the reputation of the Intelligence Ministry.[30] 'Ali Yunisi, a member of Khatami's investigative committee, became the next intelligence minister.

The Fida'iyan-i Islam and the Sa'id Imami Affair

On June 19, 1999, it was announced that Sa'id Imami (also known as Sa'id Islami), had not only been named as the ringleader in the so-called dissident murders, but that he had allegedly committed suicide in prison. IRNA reported that Imami had swallowed hair removal powder, a claim ridiculed on the streets of Tehran.[31] Accordingly, a conveniently deceased Sa'id Imami became the focal point in an investigation of what, in local parlance, became known as the "Sa'id Imami Gang," which supposedly consisted of Imami and the others arrested with him (with whom he had allegedly operated). Following the disclosure of Sa'id Imami's name, the Iranian press rushed to construct his biography. Imami had reportedly traveled to the United States in 1978 under the sponsorship of his uncle, Sultan Muhammad Itimad, Iran's military attaché in Washington.[32] Ibrahim Yazdi, foreign minister in Mehdi Bazargan's cabinet and currently head of the Iranian Freedom Movement, told the reformist daily *Arya* that Imami began study at Oklahoma State University in Stillwater, in September 1978, when he was twenty years old;[33] in 1982, he received his Bachelor of Science degree in mechanical engineering. Upon graduation, Imami worked for several months at the Iranian Interest Section in Washington, DC, followed by a year at the Islamic Republic's United Nations (UN) mission.[34] During his time in Stillwater, Imami was known for his activity on Islamic councils and, while working for Iran's UN mission, he served concurrently as secretary of the Islamic Students Association of the United States and Canada.[35] According to the reformist daily *Salam*, Imami came to the attention of future Intelligence Minister 'Ali Fallahian during the latter's secret visit to the UN in the 1980s (most likely 1983 or 1984).[36] According to Yazdi, Imami returned to Iran to join the security services in 1984.[37]

Yazdi reported that Imami entered the Intelligence Ministry during Muhammad Muhammadi Rayshahri's 1984–1989 tenure as minister (in an editorial in the June 27 edition of *Khurdad*, Rayshahri claimed that he had opposed Imami's appointment). After Fallahian became intelligence minister in 1989, he reportedly promoted Imami to a deputy-level position in the ministry. When Fallahian was replaced in 1997, Imami went from being deputy for security affairs to deputy for investigations (he was eventually replaced in that position by another appointee).[38] Although the Intelligence Ministry does not release the names of its employees for national security reasons, Imami was not an entirely unknown official. In 1996, as deputy for security affairs, he gave a speech to students at Bu 'Ali University in the Western Iranian city of Hamadan. In that speech, he claimed responsibility for the television program *Huviyat* (Identity), which was known for disparaging Iranian intellectuals. In 1999, in defiance of an Intelligence Ministry injunction, the Society of Islamic Students at Tehran's Science and Technology University screened a video of the speech to a packed auditorium.[39]

Several reformists have theorized that Intelligence Ministry officials may have killed Imami to keep him from fingering higher-ranking officials like Fallahian, who had been found guilty by a German court of organizing the 1992 assassination of four Kurdish dissidents in Berlin. Prominent reform-ist journalist (and former U.S. embassy hostage taker) 'Abbas Abdi suggested openly in an interview with *Khurdad* that in-vestigators should question Fallahian about both Imami's death and Fallahian's involvement in the dissident "serial kill-ings." Reformist papers *Salam* and *Neshat* both reiterated this demand.[40] A *Subh-i Imruz* editorial took the issue further, ques-tioning what former President Rafsanjani might have known himself and why he had appointed Fallahian to such an im-portant position as intelligence minister in the first place.[41]

Imami's funeral was attended by several well-known hardliners and Intelligence Ministry officials. Among them, the most prominent was Hojjatolislam Ruhollah Husaynian, deputy head of the Society for the Defense of Values of the Islamic Revolution (the group that coordinated Rayshahri's unsuccessful bid for the presidency in 1997). Husaynian had also previously held high-level positions in the Intelligence Ministry and is still a member of the Special Clerical Court, one of the most active hardliner bastions.[42] Speaking three months after Imami's death at the *Madrasa-yi Haqqani* semi-nary in Qum, Husaynian not only revived his claim, made previously in January 1999, that Khatami supporters such as Sa'id Hajjarian were behind the dissident killings; he also blamed Khatami's allies for Imami's death, although what motivation they may have had for his murder remains un-clear.[43] He further alluded to the possible involvement of Ayatollah Husayn 'Ali Montazeri's allies and perhaps the "Mehdi Hashemi Gang."[44]

Husaynian's speech was widely reported on by both the reformist and the hardline press. Rather than deflecting blame away from the Intelligence Ministry, the speech served to raise speculation that Husaynian was trying to protect Fallahian, under whose eight-year leadership of the ministry numerous dissidents had been killed in Iran and in Europe. The hardline official daily *Kayhan* was in the minority in specu-lating that those attacking Fallahian in the press were upset over his role as intelligence minister in crushing the Mehdi Hashemi Gang.[45] Among the most critical of Fallahian was

Akbar Ganji, a frequent contributor to the reformist *Subh-i Imruz,* and whose *Dungeon of Ghosts,* written retrospectively after these events, revealed the existence of a secret commit-tee that met to decide which dissidents the government—then headed by Rafsanjani—should eliminate. According to Ganji, the committee included Rafsanjani, Husaynian, two senior clerics, and Sa'id Imami.[46]

On April 22, 2000, Ganji was arrested and charged with ten complaints related to his reporting of and participation in a controversial Berlin conference on Iranian civil society in which reformists were videotaped together with members of illegal opposition groups. Plaintiffs against Ganji included the Intelligence Ministry, the IRGC, the hardline daily *Kayhan,* the Law Enforcement Forces, and the Headquarters for En-joining the Good and Prohibiting the Evil (the formal name of the religious "moral police," many of whose members were formerly street vigilantes loosely organized and active in the 1980s and early 1990s).[47] Upon his arrest, Ganji released a statement meant to stave off any attempt "to suicide" him, declaring, "My safety was in the hands of the Iranian authori-ties and I warn that if something happened to me, the authorities would be held responsible. . . . You can be sure that I am not about to swallow any suspect poison."[48]

In December 1999, *Subh-i Imruz* reported that some sev-enty members of the Majlis were demanding to hear the taped "confessions" of suspects arrested in the dissident murder case.[49] On January 23, the Majlis viewed the tape featuring the confessions—evidently forced—of Mustafa Kazemi (also known as Musavi Nizhad), Khusru Barati (the former airport taxi driver who had attempted to drive the writers' bus off a cliff in Armenia), Khusru Alikhani (the former chief of the Intelligence Department in Karaj), and Sa'id Imami's widow. The three men allegedly spoke of their links to foreign coun-tries, to the Israeli Mossad, and to the U.S. Central Intelligence Agency (CIA). Imami's widow described her husband as an agent of the CIA and claimed that she herself was an agent of the Federal Bureau of Investigation.[50] The three men also "confessed" to a September 1999 bombing in Mashhad that killed two people, claiming to have themselves written Fida'iyan-i Islam's statement of responsibility for that attack.[51]

Who is ultimately to blame for the dissident murders and for that of Sa'id Imami? The alleged confessions raise several possibilities:

- The "Sa'id Imami Gang" and the resurrected Fida'iyan-i Islam could be one and the same organization.
- Sa'id Imami Gang members or sympathizers might issue statements in the name of the Fida'iyan-i Islam in order to obfuscate the investigation.
- The Iranian authorities might simply be trying to pin a number of unsolved crimes on the same scapegoats. Such an action could spare the Intelligence Ministry and others closely affiliated with Supreme Leader Khamene'i the embarrassment of implication.
- Ansar-i Hizbullah might have penned the Fida'iyan-i Islam statements (Amir Farshad Ibrahimi reported that Husayn Allah-Karam was the author) in order to embarrass Khatami—by targeting Westerners at the same time that the Iranian president was seeking the highly public "dialogue of civilizations" campaign to better Iran's image abroad.

To this day, the dissident killings remain unresolved. According to the prosecutor in the case, Hojjatolislam Muhammad Niyazi (Yunisi's former deputy at the Judicial Organization of the Armed Forces), Foruhar knew at least one of his attackers. That man allegedly introduced Foruhar to some friends who, in the course of an evening's conversation, attacked their host.[52]

Meanwhile, the case remains mired in the politics of the Islamic Republic. Eight of the arrested suspects were released in April 2000 based on "clear proof" of their innocence, and others reportedly have been arrested since.[53] Husaynian, meanwhile, has sued Hamid Riza Kaviani, deputy editor of the reformist daily *Asr-i Ma* (Our Era), for alleged slander implicating him in the dissident murders.[54] Moreover, on May 9, the reformist *Ham Mihan* (Fellow Countryman) reported that a security services agent had the Foruhars' house under surveillance when the slayings occurred but was afraid to come forward, fearful for his life.[55] At a June 10 press conference, presiding judge Muhammad Niyazi indicated that he had effectively been pushed out of the loop in the investigation by Khatami and by Judiciary chairman Mahmud Hashemi-Shahrudi. Niyazi declined to discuss either the progress of the case or the number of suspects, but he flatly denied speculation that any senior religious official had issued fatwas calling for the victims' deaths, stating that such a move would be religiously impossible. He asked rhetorically, "How can a religious leader give the go ahead to stab a defenseless woman at night?"[56] Despite the marginalization of Niyazi—an indication of further efforts by Khatami to extend his authority over the Intelligence Ministry—it is not yet clear that Khatami has the power to bring the case to trial and ultimately to justice.

The Continuing Threat

Although the "Sa'id Imami Gang" and Fida'iyan-i Islam may have intended to intimidate intellectuals and reverse the general trend toward relaxing Islamic Revolutionary values in Iran, the effect of their actions was just the opposite. Indeed, the shock of the dissident murders galvanized Iranian society toward demanding the rule of law and transparency in government. Still—despite both the high visibility of the investigation surrounding the murders and the pressure groups' failure to cow the reformists—other reformist figures continued to receive threats.

Habibullah Payman, for example, leader of the Movement of Combatant Muslims and dissident intellectual who challenged the natural right of clerics to rule, received several telephoned death threats in early January 1999. Eleven months later, he was severely beaten by vigilantes.[57] While it is not clear which group specifically targeted Payman, the fact that many of the hardline pressure groups have similar patrons among the Islamic Republic's upper hierarchy makes the issue somewhat moot. Fida'iyan-i Islam allegedly sent death threats to Riza Alijani, editor of the moderate *Iran-i*

Farda (Tomorrow's Iran) monthly magazine. According to 'Izzatullah Sahabi, the magazine's publisher and a noted Islamic leftist closely associated with the Iranian Freedom Movement, the note referred to the killings of the other intellectuals and warned, "You are next, Alijani, and if you continue to give interviews to foreign radio stations, your next interview will be the last in your life."[58]

On January 5, 1999, *Zan* reported that the Fida'iyan-i Islam was prepared to take its battle beyond the borders of Iran to carry out the fatwa issued by Khomeini for the murder of Salman Rushdie.[59] This threat, while never carried out, does suggest the possibility that Iranian vigilante groups may take their terrorist activities abroad according to the will of Iran's increasingly embattled hardliners. The next day, *Hamshahri* reported the fatal stabbing of Ibrahim Zalzadeh, managing editor of the reformist *Mayar* daily.[60]

More than a year later, on February 6, 2000, Tehran's reformist *Akbar-i Iqtisad* (News of the Economy) published a Fida'iyan-i Islam announcement that the group had investigated and found guilty six Iranian government officials as the "corrupt of the earth." (According to the January 5, 1999, *Zan* report, cited above, the Fida'iyan-i Islam consists of a judicial branch overseen by three judges who "try" those opposed to the group's beliefs.[61]) The announcement promised that "the courageous members of this organization's operational unit have rolled up their sleeves and are ready for martyrdom, and in an appropriate cycle of time shall execute the verdict of Almighty God."[62]

The Shooting of Sa'id Hajjarian

In the shadow of the overwhelming victory of reformist candidates in the February 2000 first-round Majlis elections, vigilantes struck again. On the morning of March 12, 2000, an assailant shot Sa'id Hajjarian—city councilman, advisor to Khatami, and editor of the reformist daily *Subh-i Imruz*. Hajjarian had done much to earn the antipathy of Iran's radical fringe. A former deputy minister of intelligence and a specialist in psychological warfare, he had left the Intelligence

Ministry and had become a leading member of the reformist Islamic Iran Participation Front (IIPF), led by the president's brother, Muhammad Riza Khatami. As editor of *Subh-i Imruz,* Hajjarian had published Akbar Ganji's hard-hitting expose of the Intelligence Ministry, later compiled and expanded in Ganji's *Dungeon of Ghosts.* In the months preceding the shooting, he was called to appear several times to answer charges that *Subh-i Imruz* had published official secrets in its series on the dissident murders;[63] he also received death threats during the month before his murder.[64]

Suspicion for the attack immediately fell on vigilantes for several reasons. To the radical hardline fringe, Hajjarian was a hated figure for all the reasons stated above. Moreover, lead investigator Colonel Husayn Mustafi reported that the suspects' motorcycle had a 1,000 cubic centimeter (cc) engine—a significant fact, as Iranian law restricts motorcycles with engines more powerful than 250 ccs to the police, security services, paramilitary Basij, and Revolutionary Guards.[65] Nor was there a lone gunman. Two assailants on a motorcycle approached Hajjarian and one shot him in the neck, while a third distracted him.[66]

On March 20, investigators announced the arrest of six suspects in the conspiracy to kill Hajjarian, including the alleged hit man and the motorcycle driver. The IRGC Intelligence Unit carried out the arrests but turned the suspects over to the Intelligence Ministry—a disputed procedure akin to having "foxes guard the hen house," especially after the suspicious death of Sa'id Imami, which some reformists interpreted as an Intelligence Ministry attempt to silence one who knew too much.[67] The following day, the alleged hit man was identified as Sa'id Asgar, a chemistry student at Islam Azad University in Tehran (with dozens of branches across Iran, Islam Azad University is the country's equivalent of a community college).

The Supreme National Security Council warned against "rumors and malicious analysis" and, on March 22, *ash-Sharq al-Awsat* reported that Iranian authorities had warned leading reformist papers and prominent journalists not to link the Revolutionary Guards or the Basij forces to the assassination attempt. Minister of Intelligence 'Ali Yunisi declared at a March 25 news conference that the assailants had "no affiliation to any group or guild," although he admitted that one suspect worked as a guard at an IRGC facility.[68] Speculation as to the involvement of higher officials, however, was rampant. *Musharikat,* a reformist daily run by Khatami's brother, Muhammad Riza, commented, "Arresting only the hit men may not shed light on the depth of the catastrophe. There is a need to aim at their commanders."[69] An unnamed source told *ash-Sharq al-Awsat* that the killing had been organized by the Islam Combatants Corps, a group reportedly composed of IRGC officers.[70] But London-based journalist 'Ali Nurizadeh reported three other theories being discussed: first, that at least one assailant was connected with the Sa'id Imami Gang; second, that the security services had targeted Hajjarian in revenge for his revelations that led to the jailing of Brigadier-General Muhammad Riza Naqdi, a senior police official charged with the torture of a political detainee; and third, that a pressure group linked with Rafsanjani may have ordered Hajjarian's hit in order to protect the former president from Hajjarian's repeated calls for an inquiry into the sources of Rafsanjani's wealth.[71]

Faced with widespread speculation of Revolutionary Guard involvement, the authorities struck back with arrests that suggested the Hajjarian shooting was the result of a dispute within the reformist camp. On April 15, authorities in Zanjan arrested Ahmad Hakimipur, a reformist colleague of Hajjarian's on the Tehran City Council, and himself the editor of a local paper in Zanjan. Two weeks earlier, IRNA reported that Hakimipur had known one of the suspects in the Hajjarian shooting, Muhammad 'Ali Muqaddami.[72] Hakimipur was a member of the Central Committee of the Assembly of the Imam's Line Forces, a reformist faction taking its name from the vigilante group Students Following the Line of the Imam.[73] This fueled some hardliners' speculation that the shooting of Hajjarian was motivated by a power struggle among the reformists. Iran's official hardline Voice of the Islamic Republic speculated that the assassination attempt was part of a larger conspiracy involving Iranian reformers, Furqan, the Mehdi Hashemi Gang, Sa'id Imami, the United States, and the Iraqi-sponsored Mujahidin-i Khalq Organization—an assertion ridiculous to all but the most conspiratorially minded.[74] Ansar-i Hizbullah's Masud Dehnamaki told *Subh-i Imruz* that "extremist reformers are seeking to get rid of certain individuals connected to the Second of Khordad [reformist] Front and this is why Hajjarian may have been targeted by them." In the same interview, however, he contradicted himself, adding that Khatami's allies "are overlooking the two-decade Islamic Revolution, and launch counter-revolutionary slogans. They should know that their requests are unlawful and beyond the reformists' claims. Hence, they should pay the price for this."[75]

A scenario involving Hakimipur would be consistent in part with the murder of the Foruhars, who were most likely ambushed with the assistance of someone known to them, given that they were murdered inside their own home without any sign of forced entry. But Hakimipur had publicly acknowledged his extremely limited relationship with the suspect soon after the latter's involvement in the assassination attempt became known. Within five days Hakimipur was free on bail, and he was eventually exonerated by the Revolutionary Court.

The Intelligence Ministry under Siege

Not two weeks passed before the investigation into the Hajjarian shooting became mired in a power struggle between the pro-Khamene'i Intelligence Ministry and the Ministry of Interior, which is far closer to Khatami and the reformists. Muhammad Riza Khatami's political movement, the IIPF, accused the Intelligence Ministry of intervening in the investigation for the purpose of squelching any opportunity that reformists in other state organs might seize upon to interrogate the assailants, as "some of those arrested have ties there [to the Intelligence Ministry]." In the same statement, the IIPF alleged that "the suspects also have links with certain personalities who advocate violence against reformers."[76] On March 26, 2000, Vice President Massumeh Ibtikar (the former spokeswoman for the U.S. embassy hostage takers) publicly linked Hajjarian's shooting to both the 1998 dissident murders and the 1999 police and vigilante attack on the Tehran University dormitory.[77] That same day, Khatami urged Intelligence Minister 'Ali Yunisi to act quickly, writing, "This evil [terrorism] will engulf us and demolish everything like termites."[78]

The following month, the Assembly of the Imam's Line Forces—the group to which Hakimipur belonged—further tied the suspects to Iran's multifaceted security apparatus. The Assembly alleged in a statement that the hardline-dominated Council of Guardians had previously appointed several of the suspects as supervisors in the February 2000 first-round Majlis elections. According to the statement, the suspects had come to the attention of the council because of their prominent role in the *komiteh* religious police squads—the name assumed by the informal vigilante "moral police" of the 1980s and early 1990s after their absorption into the Interior Ministry during the Rafsanjani administration.[79]

The investigation proceeded quickly—too quickly, according to some reformers. On March 25, Yunisi announced the arrests of ten people and angrily denied Muhammad Riza Khatami's charges that the Intelligence Ministry was involved in a cover-up.[80] Adding to the speculation that the government had engaged in a speedy trial to prevent the investigation from expanding beyond the actual hit men, a report surfaced about a bizarre incident involving an Iran Air airplane on March 15, 2000. Three days after the shooting of Hajjarian, a regularly scheduled Iran Air flight from Kirman to Tehran reportedly experienced a navigational error and flew several hundred miles in the opposite direction, landing instead in Karachi, Pakistan. The mystery of how the pilot failed to notice the unfamiliar terrain below him on a route through clear desert skies remains unexplained (Tehran lies at the foot of a 10,000-foot-high mountain range, while Karachi is a port).

Suspicions intensified when, on April 18, the official newspaper *Iran* quoted an unnamed Majlis deputy as saying, "The person who got off at Karachi was called Qasimi and had an active role in the attack [on Hajjarian]."[81] Meanwhile, Sadiqeh Vasmaqi, spokeswoman for the Tehran City Council, issued a statement in early April indicating that threats against the City Council's reformist legislators continued: "The head of the Tehran City Council received death threats a few days after the assassination attempt on Sa'id Hajjarian. . . . The death squad relayed a message to Chairman Rahmatullah Khusravi of the Council, singling him out as the next murder victim."[82]

In early April, a jurisdictional dispute between the Intelligence Ministry and the Judiciary became public. On April 3, Abbas 'Ali Alizadeh, Tehran's Judiciary chief, demanded that the Intelligence Ministry hand over the suspects in the Hajjarian shooting, declaring such a move necessary "to prevent any conceivable punishment, threats, pressure, or injury to the accused."[83] Yunisi released the suspects to the Judiciary under protest. He complained publicly to Khatami that the transfer of the suspects and the investigation file from the Intelligence Ministry to the Judiciary "deprived the Information [Intelligence] Ministry of exercising its legal responsibilities."[84]

Akbar Ganji publicly ridiculed Yunisi's claim that, as the assailants had personal motivation to attack Hajjarian, there was no reason to assume any conspiracy. Ganji told *Subh-i Imruz* that Yunisi's explanation was "not becoming [of] the status of the intelligence minister. . . . Personal motivation exists when the two sides know each other and one has violated the right of the other."[85] With regard to the March 12 attack, Ganji explained,

> The terrorists did not know Sa'id Hajjarian. They were a known 'operational circle' and they had carried out many operations in the past. Probably the theoreticians of the 'slaughter-therapy' placed an order with the 'military wing' for assassination of Sa'id Hajjarian. Therefore, the eyes should not be directed at a few terrorists and their circle, and one should look for the rear of the criminals. The main criminals are individuals who theorize violence from pub-

lic pulpits and in private circles clarify the examples of their talks by mentioning names.[86]

Ganji went on to say that the likely suspects were associates of Qum's Madrasa-yi Haqqani, a seminary with a key role in managing the Intelligence Ministry.[87] According to *Hamshahri*, three of the Islamic Republic's four intelligence ministers received their education at Haqqani and were students there of Ayatollah Muhammad Taqi Misbah Yazdi, a leading hardline ideologue who regularly preaches that violence is a legitimate means to uphold religious values (Misbah Yazdi is also the brother of former Iranian Judiciary Chief Muhammad Yazdi).[88] In addition, Haqqani graduates dominate the Special Clerical Court, and Ghulamhusayn Rahbapur, the chief judge of the Revolutionary Courts until May 2000, was also trained at the seminary.[89] Ayatollah Sadiq Khalkhali, the former Fida'iyan-i Islam chairman who now places himself in the reformist camp, claimed in 1999 that the Madrasa-yi Haqqani had become a breeding ground for religiously motivated murder plots.[90]

Indeed, the central position of the Madrasa-yi Haqqani raises an important question: *Can the seeming impunity with which the Sa'id Imami Gang, the revived Fida'iyan-i Islam, and Intelligence Ministry vigilante groups carry out successful attacks on their targets be traced to a relatively small circle of powerful officials that enjoy high-level clerical support?* Given their strong and influential presence in the Judiciary, the question of whether Haqqani graduates can or ever would be brought to trial for murders religiously sanctioned by Misbah Yazdi and his protégés is also significant.

The Trial of Sa'id Asgar

The trial of the suspects in the attack on Hajjarian—who were eventually turned over by the Intelligence Ministry—opened on April 25, 2000, and was presided over by Judge Husayn Razghandi—considered a hardliner by IRNA.[91] The trial lasted less than one month. On May 17, the court sentenced Asgar, the trigger man, to fifteen years of imprisonment, and his accomplices to terms ranging between four and ten years.

Although on the surface, such speedy justice might seem a positive development, the trial left many issues unresolved. For instance, it came out during the proceedings that Muhsin Majidi, a guard at an IRGC base, acquired the security services–issue motorcycle from another individual, but the court left unanswered the question of how the latter had acquired the motorcycle.[92] The trial also revealed that the suspects viewed themselves as a cell and had attempted to carry out two previous assassinations—one of a minor IRGC official and another of an electrician.[93] In choosing Hajjarian as a target, Asgar revealed that the group had sought a fatwa from clerics in Shahr-i Rayy (a historically important village on the southern edge of Tehran), although Asgar later denied this.[94] Such a procedure would be similar to an alleged Fida'iyan-i Islam plot to assassinate six government officials, which also reportedly involved the issuing of a February 2000 fatwa.[95] Although the two fatwas may not be linked, if both reports are true they point to a common modus operandi among hardline vigilante groups: the acquisition of rulings by extremist religious figures to justify their actions. It is in this context that control of the Madrasa-yi Haqqani becomes so crucial, in that the hardliners use the religious legitimacy bestowed by the seminary to help fulfill their distinctly non-religious actions.

The speed of the trial caused leading opposition figures to charge that a cover-up was being perpetrated by a short-circuiting of the investigation.[96] Ghulam 'Ali Riyahi, a lawyer who represented Hajjarian against hardliner complaints relating to *Subh-i Imruz*'s investigative articles about the dissident murders, called for the investigation to continue in order to "uncover the main proponents of the assassination attempt."[97]

A Fatwa against Khatami?

Beginning on April 23, 2000, the hardline-dominated Judiciary began to close down the majority of Iran's reformist newspapers and journals. By April 27 sixteen had closed (in 1999, the Judiciary had acted against only one or two newspapers; thus, the magnitude of the April 2000 closures came as a shock to Iranians). The inauguration of a new reformist-dominated Majlis in May 2000 did little to mitigate the power struggle in Iran. Rather than accept their defeat in the Majlis elections, the hardliners regrouped and intensified their efforts to salvage their own vision of the values of the Islamic Revolution in the face of popular rebuke.

Then, in May, an informant leaked a plot to assassinate Khatami himself. The would-be assassin, a member of the IRGC and a Khatami bodyguard, allegedly approached Ayatollah Husayn Nuri-Hamadani for a fatwa, but Nuri-Hamadani referred him to the more prominent Ayatollah Muhammad Fazl-Lankani to sanction the assassination.[98] It was Lankani's son who supposedly alerted the authorities, perhaps saving Iran from the civil chaos that surely would have followed Khatami's murder.

Why Provoke a Crisis?

Certain vigilante groups might think provoking a crisis to be in their interests, even at the risk of precipitating societal turmoil. But more than half of Iran's population was born or came of age after the Islamic Revolution, and consequently they have no memory of the shah's regime with its endemic corruption and oppression. Accordingly, when young Iranians see the same problems manifested in the Islamic Republic, they blame the only government they know, especially the hardline clergy. Indeed, with the youth largely opposed to the austerity preached by a wealthy clerical class, there is little chance that hardline politicians will be able to win at the ballot box in the near future. Alternatively, an outbreak of violence precipitated by vigilantes might provide Iran's security services with an excuse to crack down, roll back reforms, and curtail civil liberties, all in the name of restoring order and maintaining national security. Although such a scenario would likely harm Iran's economy, society, and international standing, a small minority of vigilante hardliners and their clerical and Revolutionary Guard supporters might deem the trade-off as necessary to maintain their grip on power.

Notes

1. Afshin Valinejad, "Former U.S. Hostages Receive Death Threat in Iran," Associated Press Worldstream, November 9, 1998.

2. "Fada'yan-e Eslam Group Says It Attacked U.S. Tourists," *al-Hayat*, November 23, 1998, in BBC Summary of World Broadcasts, November 25, 1998 (ME/D3393/MED). The son of a prominent Tehran intellectual claimed that, despite all the press coverage about Fida'iyan-i Islam, businessmen rivals of 'Ali Sabzalian—the host of the Americans' trip and the former head of the Islamic Republic's Interest Section at the Pakistani embassy in Washington—organized the attack in order to embarrass Sabzalian (Interview by author in Tehran, July 1999). Even if true, such an explanation does not necessarily negate the possibility that Fida'iyan-i Islam had indeed reemerged, as politics and business interests are often intimately intertwined. For example, Foreign Ministry spokesman Hamid Riza Asefi reported that the Iranian government had actually granted the American businessmen their visas to encourage them to pressure the U.S. Congress to oppose sanctions against Iran. Indeed, hardline sponsors of pressure groups often have their own economic concerns. Many officials with pecuniary interests in the shadowy *bunyads* (revolutionary foundations) have little desire to see liberalization toward the West, especially if Western investment would increase competition and thus the demand for economic transparency.

3. "Iranian Official Condemns Attack on Bus Carrying American Tourists, Associated Press, November 24, 1998.

4. Afshin Valinejad, "Militants Defy Khatami by Backing the Attack on U.S. Businessmen," Associated Press Worldstream, November 27, 1998.

5. For an account of the group, see Michael Rubin, "Iran's 'Dialogue of Civilizations'—A First-Hand Account," *Middle East Quarterly*, March 2000, pp. 31–38.

6. "A Report on the Case of the Serial Killings After One Year," *Payam-i Imruz*, November 1999, p. 19, provided by Iran News internet service.

7. Nahid Musavi, "A Review of [the] Serial Murders," *Zanan*, no. 58, December 1999, online at www.netiran.com/Htdocs/Clippings/Dpolitics/991228XXDP03.html

8. "Tehran says 'Zionists' Implicated in Murder of Opposition Leader," Agence France Presse, November 24, 1998.

9. Ervand Abrahamian, *Iran between Two Revolutions* (Princeton: Princeton University Press, 1982), pp. 257–258.

10. Ibid., pp. 501–502.

11. Ibid., p. 504.

12. Musavi, "A Review of [the] Serial Murders."

13. Ibid.

14. Ibid.

15. "Iranian Intellectuals Appeal for Freedom," Associated Press, October 25, 1994; "A Report on the Case of the Serial Killings After One Year"; *Fath*, January 19, 2000, translation provided by SMCCDI; Musavi, "A Review of [the] Serial Murders."

16. Musavi, "A Review of [the] Serial Murders."

17. Jacki Lyden and Craig Windham, "Writers in Iran," National Public Radio's *All Things Considered*, June 1, 1997, transcript no. 97060105-216.

18. Musavi, "A Review of [the] Serial Murders."

19. Elaine Sciolino, "Frightening Reassurances in Iran: Some Officials Ran a Hit Squad. It's Over. Still Worried?" *New York Times*, January 10, 1999, Section 4, Page 5.

20. Douglas Jehl, "Killing of 3 Rebel Writers Turns Hope to Fear in Iran," *New York Times*, December 14, 1998, p. A6.

21. Ibid.

22. Musavi, "A Review of [the] Serial Murders"; "New Secrets about Serial Killings," *Intikhab*, January 31, 2000, p. 3, online at www.netiran.com/Htdocs/Clippings/DPolitics/200131XXDP01.html

23. Musavi, "A Review of [the] Serial Murders."

24. Scott Peterson, "Iran's Arrests of Intelligence Officers May Be Watershed," *Christian Science Monitor*, January 8, 1999, p. 8.

25. "Iran Security Minister Resigns; Jannati Calls for Khatami's Removal," *ash-Sharq al-Awsat*, January 6, 1999, p. 1, in FBIS-NES-99-006.

26. "Four More Iranian Intelligence Agents Arrested over Killings," Deutsche Press Agentur, February 22, 1999.

27. "Iranian Services Disagree Whether to Show Killers' 'Confessions' on TV," Agence France Presse, January 26, 2000.

28. Musavi, "A Review of [the] Serial Murders."

29. Ibid.

30. "Information Minister's Letter of Resignation," Vision of the Islamic Republic Network 1, February 9, 1999, in BBC Summary of World Broadcasts, February 11, 1999 (ME/D3456/MED).

31. Interviews by author in Tehran, July and August 1999.

32. Musavi, "A Review of [the] Serial Murders."

33. 'Ali Riza Nurizadeh, *Guzarish-i Qatliha va I'tarafat-i Sa'id Imami* (Report on the murders and confessions of Sa'id Imami) (Spanga, Sweden: Baran, 1999), pp. 50–51.

34. "A Report on the Case of the Serial Killings after One Year"; Nurizadeh, p. 52.

35. Nurizadeh, p. 52.

36. "Forouhar Assassin Gets Suicided," *Iran Brief*, July 6, 1999.

37. "A Report on the Case of the Serial Killings After One Year."

38. Ibid. For a detailed history of the Intelligence Ministry, see Nurizadeh, pp. 79 99.

39. "Iranian Student Group Shows Filmed Speech of Saeed Emami," *Tehran Times* (internet edition), December 1, 1999, online at www.tehrantimes.com

40. Abbas Samii, "Fallahian in from the Cold," Radio Free Europe/Radio Liberty (RFE/RL) *Iran Report* 2, no. 27, July 7, 1999.

41. *Subh-i Imruz*, December 16, 1999. Translation provided by SMCCDI.

42. Samii, "Fallahian in from the Cold."

43. "Sukhinan-i Husaynian dar Madrasa-yi Haqqani" (Sermons delivered at the Madrasa'yi Haqqani) in Nurizadeh, p. 256.

44. Abbas Samii, "Husseinian Protecting Fallahian?" RFE/RL *Iran Report* 2, no. 38, September 27, 1999.

45. Ibid.

46. Robert Fisk, "Revealed: Role of a President in the Murder of His People," *The Independent*, March 8, 2000, p. 1.

47. "Akbar Ganji Sent to Prison," *Tehran Times* (internet edition), April 23, 2000, online at www.tehrantimes.com

48. "Suicide is not for me—Ganji," *Subh-i Imruz*, April 24, 2000. Translation provided by SMCCDI.

49. "Iranian MPs Demand to See Taped Confession in Murder Case," Agence France Presse, December 22, 1999.

50. "Iran 'Rogue Agents' Admit U.S., Israeli Ties: Press," Reuters, January 24, 2000.

51. "Iranian Services Disagree Whether to Show Killers' 'Confessions' on TV."

52. "A Report on the Case of the Serial Killings after One Year."

53. Ali Akbar Dareini, "Iran's Judiciary Frees 8 Serial Killings Suspects, Arrests Others," Associated Press Worldstream, April 27, 2000.

54. "Judge Suing Journalist for Book on Slaying of Intellectuals," Agence France Presse, April 3, 2000.

55. "Eyewitness Colonel Lives in Fear for His Life!" *Ham Mihan*, May 9, 2000. Translation provided by SMCCDI.

56. "Niyazi Pulled off Murder Probe," *Iran Times*, June 16, 2000.

57. Afshin Valinejad, "Iran Prosecutor: Several Murder Suspects Freed, Others at Large," Associated Press Worldstream, January 20, 1999.

58. "Radicals Threaten Magazine Editor in Iran," *Boston Globe*, January 16, 1999, p. A5.

59. Michael Theodoulou, "'Rogue' Agents Killed Dissidents, Iran Says," *The Times* (London), January 6, 1999.

60. *Hamshahri*, February 6, 2000. Translation provided by SMCCDI.

61. Theodoulou, "'Rogue' Agents Killed Dissidents, Iran Says."

62. "Fada'ian of Genuine Muhammadan Islam Threaten to Carry Out Sentences against Six Corrupt of the Earth," *Akbar-i Iqtisad* (internet edition), February 6, 2000.

63. Kianouche Dorraine, "Leading Reformist Wounded in Assassination Bid in Tehran," Agence France Presse, March 12, 2000.

64. "Author of Death Threat against Hajjarian Arrested: Press," Agence France Presse, March 16, 2000.

65. 'Ali Nurizadeh, "Assassination Attempt Will Not Browbeat Iran Reformers," *Mideast Mirror*, March 14, 2000.

66. "Hajjarian Assassination Attempt Trial, First Session," April 25, 2000, Part 1, www.iranmania.com/news/hajjarian/trial1/default.asp

67. Jim Muir, "Row over Reformist's Shooting," BBC News internet edition, April 6, 2000, online at news6.thdo.bbc.co.uk/hi/english/world/middle%5Feast/newsid%5F704000/704074.stm

68. "Information Minister Gives Update on Assassination Attempt Investigations," Islamic Republic News Agency (IRNA), March 25, 2000.

69. Mehrdad Balali, "Iran Identifies 'Hitman' in Reformer's Shooting," Reuters, March 21, 2000.

70. "Revolutionary Guards Faction Said Behind Shooting of Iranian Reformer," *Mideast Mirror*, March 22, 2000; Balali, "Iran Identifies 'Hitman' in Reformer's Shooting."

71. Nurizadeh, "Assassination Attempt Will Not Browbeat Iran Reformers."

72. "Iran Paper on 'Infiltration' into Both Political Currents," IRNA, April 2, 2000, in FBIS-NES-2000-0402; "Iran Reformists Face Threats and More Annulments of Poll Wins," *Mideast Mirror* (from *Ash-Sharq al-Awsat*), April 17, 2000.

73. "Guardian Council–Appointed Supervisors Turned Killer," *Hamshahri*, April 19, 2000. Translation provided by SMCCDI.

74. "Assassinations, Conspiracies Seen," Voice of the Islamic Republic of Iran Radio 1, April 1, 2000, in BBC Worldwide Monitoring, through GlobalNews Bank, online at www.newsbank..com

75. *Subh-i Imruz*, April 4, 2000. Translation provided by SMCCDI.

76. Mehrdad Balali, "Iran Reformers Rap Probe of Reformist's Shooting," Reuters, March 23, 2000.

77. "Official: Shooting of Reformer, 1998 Dissident Murders Are Linked," Associated Press, March 26, 2000.

78. "Iran President Warns Terrorism Could Destroy Nation 'Like Termites'," Agence France Presse, March 26, 2000.

79. "Guardian Council–Appointed Supervisors Turned Killers."

80. "10 Held in Attack on Official, Iran Says," *Los Angeles Times*, March 26, 2000, p. A28.

81. "Suspected Attacker of Iranian Reformist Escaped to Pakistan, Says Iran Newspaper," Agence France Presse, April 18, 2000.

82. *Azad*, April 6, 2000. Translation provided by SMCCDI.

83. "Iran Court Seeks Custody of Shooting Suspects," Reuters, April 3, 2000.

84. "Khatami–Younesi Letter," IRNA, May 4, 2000.

85. "Theoreticians of 'Slaughter Therapy' Placed Order with 'Military Wing,'" *Subh-i Imru*, March 29, 2000, pp. 1, 8.

86. Ibid.

87. Wilfried Buchta, *Who Rules Iran? The Structure of Power in the Islamic Republic* (Washington, DC: The Washington Institute for Near East Policy and Konrad Adenauer Stiftung, 2000), p. 166.

88. "Iran: Dissident Sorush Says Hajjarian Victim of 'Fascistic' Reading of Religion," *'Asr-i Azadigan* (internet edition), April 3, 2000, in BBC Worldwide Monitoring, April 4, 2000.

89. "Theoreticians of 'Slaughter-Therapy' Placed Order with 'Military Wing.'"

90. Geneive Abdo, "Fatwa Plan to Kill Iranian President," *The Guardian*, May 31, 2000, p. 15.

91. "Judge Razqandi to Handle Hajjarian's Court Case," IRNA, April 2, 2000.

92. "Hajjarian Assassination Attempt Trial, Second Session," May 3, 2000, Part 4, www.iranmania.com/news/hajjarian/trail2/trial2c.asp

93. "Hajjarian Assassination Attempt Trial, First Session," April 25, 2000, Part 2, www.iranmania.com/news/hajjarian/trial1a.asp

94. "Hajjarian Assassination Attempt Trial, First Session," April 25, 2000, Part 3, www.iranmania.com/news/hajjarian/trial1b.asp

95. "Fada'ian of Genuine Muhammadan Islam Threaten to Carry out Sentences against Six Corrupt of the Earth."

96. "Politician Who Identified a Suspect in the Hajjarian Case Arrested, Say Family," Agence France Presse, April 15, 2000.

97. "Not Guns Nor Killers, Find the Real Culprits," *Iran*, May 18, 2000.

98. Abdo, p. 15.

Chapter 5

Conclusions

Vigilante groups have long influenced Iranian politics during times of domestic and ideological uncertainty. Seldom has this influence been good for the vast majority of Iranians, let alone for U.S. and European policymakers and businessmen. Rather, the composite membership of vigilante groups—numbering perhaps just a few hundred men out of a population of nearly 70 million—has managed to push Iran toward domestic instability, autocracy, and xenophobia. As the nascent Islamic Republic debated its new constitution in 1979, a few dozen students seized the U.S. embassy, whipping up public passion and marginalizing the more moderate and even democratic revolutionary factions. The constitution adopted in the wake of the U.S. embassy seizure provided for a paper democracy, under which the expression of Iranian popular will is subject to many checks by clerical bodies. More than three years into President Muhammad Khatami's administration, it is unclear whether he will be able to peacefully fulfill his popular mandate, as leaders of many power centers in the country remain aligned against him.

Vigilante groups are not a new phenomenon in Iran; they have been active for a century. Before the Islamic Revolution, they remained largely an opposition force; under the Islamic Republic, however, they receive support at the highest levels. Although the groups are a sometimes-convenient tool through which to carry out government policy, events of the past two decades have repeatedly demonstrated that the Iranian government is unable to control the vigilantes or to permanently stamp them out when their activities become inconvenient.

115

Who Are the Vigilantes?

Many pressure groups are currently active in Iran; Ansar-i Hizbullah, Fida'iyan-i Islam, and the "Sa'id Imami Gang" are the most prominent. They aspire to common goals, although Ansar-i Hizbullah usually relies on mobs drawn from hardline, disaffected war veterans, while the operations of Fida'iyan-i Islam and the Sa'id Imami Gang tend to be more covert and professional.

Despite their differences, it remains unclear how closely related many of these groups may be to one other. For instance, it is quite possible that Ministry of Intelligence operatives who engaged in the 1998 murders of Iranian dissidents coordinated their activities to some extent with the leadership of Ansar-i Hizbullah. After all, the leadership of Ansar-i Hizbullah includes high-ranking IRGC officers, for whom contacts with Intelligence Ministry counterparts would be natural. Moreover, many of the attacks perpetrated by Ansar-i Hizbullah vigilantes indicate a close working relationship with senior Law Enforcement Forces officers and other security service officials. While the Sa'id Imami Gang and Ansar-i Hizbullah seem to have separate but mutually sympathetic membership, other groups, like the shadowy Fida'iyan-i Islam, may simply exist as fronts to inflate the collective size and strength of Iranian vigilantism in the public imagination.

Front groups would also be a convenient means by which to obfuscate the culpability of individuals who may one day be held accountable for their crimes in court, as multiple claims of responsibility can obscure the ultimate source of a pressure-group operation. Vigilante groups, after all, exist to achieve individual or core-group policy objectives by any means necessary, while simultaneously providing for plausible deniability by the political sponsorship. Thus far, Iranian courts have refused to try the highest-ranking officials for involvement in the murder of dissidents in Iran and abroad, or for allowing the 1999 attack on Tehran University's Amirabad dormitory and subsequently on universities across the country. But reformist trends indicate that such trials remain a possibility if President Khatami's allies can gain greater control over the Judiciary, Intelligence Ministry, and security services.

Most vigilante group members have never left Iran, and they have little knowledge of, and even less experience with, the world around them. Many appear to come from traditional, religious, and impoverished families, and all seem to pursue rather utopian views of an Islamic society centered on a faultless Supreme Jurisconsult. In this regard, the fight against the "weak impulses" and pragmatic statecraft takes precedence for the vigilantes over the promotion of a precise ideology. Thus, Ansar-i Hizbullah members, for example, are anything but monolithic in their views concerning the economy and the practice of politics, although they are united in a nihilistic belief that reformism is "evil" and must be combated.

In addition, memories from the Iran–Iraq War years remain strongly impressed on the leadership of the various Iranian vigilante groups. Their xenophobia—and particularly their anti-Americanism—derive not so much from U.S. support for the shah as from U.S. support for Iraq during that period.[1] Although the pressure groups perceive U.S. support for Iraq to have been more substantive than it actually was, such a distinction is irrelevant to those who experienced first-hand the horrors of an exceptionally brutal war.

Vigilante Group Operations: Implications for Iran

Although vigilante groups will likely survive with or without support from high-level government officials, it is the patronage of men in the highest clerical ranks that allows them to operate actively. Indeed, the very existence of a group like Ansar-i Hizbullah mocks the rule of law—the achievement of which has become the stated goal of many reformists in the Iranian government as well as critics not yet allowed to participate in Iran's limited democracy.

There is every reason to believe that vigilante groups operate under the sponsorship of high government officials and government ministries. After all, three years into President Khatami's administration, no member of a pressure group has yet come to trial. Likewise, the supposedly "rogue" Intelligence Ministry agents accused of murdering numerous writers and intellectuals remain untried, while an official investigation is seemingly hindered from considering the culpability of prominent officials; former Deputy Minister of Intelligence Sa'id Imami died in prison, and his colleagues have yet to appear in court for the dissident murders. Similarly, no members of Ansar-i Hizbullah have been jailed for their role in the unprovoked July 1999 attack on the Tehran University dormitory. Masud Dehnamaki and Husayn Allah-Karam continue to organize, while other pressure-group members, like Habibullah Asgarawladi, remain firmly ensconced in recognized political factions. Iranian authorities have claimed that Sa'id Hajjarian's now-imprisoned assailants were not members of pressure groups; although many reformists have speculated that their quick trial was an attempt to preempt an in-depth investigation.

Moreover, Ansar-i Hizbullah and factions within the paramilitary Basij forces continue to agitate for the murder of British author Salman Rushdie—despite declarations from Khatami and Foreign Minister Kamal Kharrazi that Iran would no longer seek to enforce Ayatollah Ruhollah Khomeini's call for Rushdie's death—and Khatami and Supreme Leader 'Ali Khamene'i appear unwilling or unable to check the threats and operations of the vigilante groups that violate agreements and treaties.

The apparent immunity of vigilantes to the wheels of justice has slowed reform by intimidating proponents of change. In the year following the Ansar-i Hizbullah attack on the Tehran University dormitory, the silent majority of students expressed fear for their safety should they rally or speak publicly in defense of civil liberties.[2] Indeed, the peaceful evolution of Iranian society, transparent and accountable government, and political stability depend upon reining in what are, in effect, Khamene'i's "brownshirts."

By impeding real reform, vigilante group activity hinders even the strengthening of Iran's deteriorating economy. Qurban 'Ali Qandahari, a Majlis deputy from Gurgan (in north-central Iran) whose seat was eliminated by redistricting before the February 2000 elections, has observed, "Pressure groups are the main obstacle to the return to the homeland of Iranians living outside the country."[3] Clearly, the infusion of Iranian expatriate capital and brain power would benefit the Iranian economy—provided that other institutional impediments, such as corruption and gross bureaucratic inefficiency, did not interfere. But vigilante groups stand in the way of such a basic step.

Still, Iranian civil society has at least matured to the point at which the reformist press, when allowed to publish, recognizes and addresses the problems of pressure groups, albeit in a necessarily restrained manner. Reformist columnist Hasan Yusifi Ishkaviri, for example, once rebutted Intelligence Minister 'Ali Yunisi's declaration that "pressure groups are not fed or supported by any official source," by assuring the minister not to worry about press inquiries. Ishkaviri wrote, "We are not planning to ask where they are organized, and where they get their weapons and radios from, and furthermore, why their criminal, discretionary, and violence-seeking activities have not been prevented in the course of the past twenty years."[4] More recently, *Bayan* columnist Mutaza Nawruzi responded to repeated hardline declarations that the only pressure groups operating are those belonging to foreign conspiracies: "Conspiracy is worse than murder, because conspiracy is the beginning of repeated bloodshed. . . . Blaming such [terrorist] actions on foreign mercenaries and unclean foreign hands is like hiding one's head in the snow for fear of the hunter."[5]

Implications for the United States

Iran's pressure groups pose unique challenges to U.S. policymakers and remain important to the United States for four primary reasons:

1) Vigilante groups pose a threat to stability in Iran;
2) Vigilante groups undermine moderation;

3) The Iranian government's tolerance for vigilantism undercuts the legitimacy of Iran's diplomatic commitments; and

4) Hardliner support for vigilantism would make a resumption of normal relations impossible, for it would pose a potential threat to any American diplomats posted to Iran.

Indeed, the Iranian government uses the presence of pressure groups both to control foreign visitors and as an excuse for not participating in Khatami's "dialogue of civilizations." According to the U.S. State Department, the United States offers Iranians well over 20,000 visas per year; Iran, according to its own statistical yearbooks, grants Americans fewer than 1,000 visas.[6] Iranians often argue that they cannot allow Americans greater access to their country for security reasons and for the sake of the visitors' own safety; the November 1998 Fida'iyan-i Islam attack on the busload of American tourists highlighted that problem. Likewise, Iran is not willing to allow a visiting U.S. consular official the opportunity to expedite the visa process by conducting interviews in Iran (or even on Iran's Persian Gulf island of Kish, where rules concerning foreigners are more relaxed). After all, such an official would be a natural target for vigilantes who are opposed to any American presence in Iran. But Iranians will never become accustomed to hosting Americans if Iranian authorities continue to restrict visits not only from government emissaries but from academics and tourists. One of the likely benefits of any rapprochement between Tehran and Washington is a resumption of diplomatic ties and normalized relations. Americans had a long history in Iran before the Revolution; in 1978, almost 45,000 Americans lived there.[7] But American businessmen, diplomats, and tourists will never be able to travel safely in Iran if hardline government officials continue to support anti-American vigilantism.

Moreover, if the Iranian government is not willing or able to control vigilante groups and guarantee safety for visitors, then it will not be a credible partner for meaningful diplomatic negotiations. No amount of people-to-people dialogue will change this reality, for it is not the Iranian population that obstructs the development of closer ties, but rather the government officials who sponsor the vigilante groups. Thus, the existence and activity of such groups will continue to be the most accurate barometer for gauging how effectively the moderate elements within the Iranian government have consolidated power.

The American Dilemma

In many ways, the problems posed for U.S. policymakers by Iran's vigilante groups are parallel to those raised by the Iranian sponsorship of terrorism. In dealing with such challenges, U.S. policymakers have tried to determine the extent to which violence and terror derive from factions and power circles in the official governing structure—like the IRGC—and to what extent they derive from the Iranian government as a whole, including Iranian moderates. In this regard, Washington has sometimes sought to differentiate between the Iranian government and individuals within the Islamic Republic who might promote acts of terror. For example, at an October 5, 1999, briefing, State Department spokesman James Rubin carefully avoided placing blame on Iran's government for the attack on the Khobar U.S. military barracks in Saudi Arabia. He did reveal that Washington had "specific information with respect to the involvement of Iranian government officials," and that the United States "sought a commitment from the government of Iran to support bringing those responsible to justice."[8] Yet, the Iranian government was unresponsive to the U.S. request for cooperation in the investigation.

Making the distinction between the Iranian government and the perpetrators of vigilantism is a flawed approach. Even if violations of international norms are conducted by only a few individuals or organizations in the government, the failure of the reformist Khatami administration to pursue the investigations that follow those violations belies either the administration's internal weakness or its lack of desire to act in accordance with its own rhetoric. Against the public relations image that reformist Iranian politicians have sought to cultivate, such an official position also demonstrates that the continued isolation of the Islamic Republic by the United States may, in fact, be the best policy. A week after Rubin's press conference, Ambassador Michael Sheehan, State Department coordinator for counterterrorism, singled out the involvement of the IRGC and the Intelligence Ministry for their support of terrorism—while making clear that Washington would hold the entire Iranian government responsible for the action of any of its constituent parts. He announced, "There cannot be a [U.S.] lifting of the sanctions . . . or an improvement in relations until Iran takes meaningful steps to end its support for terrorism and cooperate in the fight against terrorism."[9]

Concerning Iranian vigilante groups, the U.S. government should maintain the posture of holding the Iranian government accountable for the entirety of Iran's actions. Some might argue that the activities of the vigilante groups are of no legitimate concern to U.S. policymakers, but this is a dangerous posture. Groups like Ansar-i Hizbullah and the Sa'id Imami Gang appear to receive support from the highest levels of the Iranian government, and their continued activity therefore strikes at the heart of Iran's diplomatic credibility. It is irrelevant that only a small proportion of the Iranian political and clerical elite support vigilantism and violence in the pursuit of policy; Iranian history shows that minority support, when powerful enough, can sustain hardline pressure groups that, in turn, have a track record of political influence greatly disproportionate to their numbers.

Although the European Union might continue to advocate a "comprehensive dialogue," the successor to its discredited policy of "critical dialogue," such an approach necessarily overlooks the root problems in Iranian society, and may therefore actually impede efforts to improve Iran's relations with the outside world. Dialogue and cultural exchange are useful, but they are no substitutes for accountability. Iranian vigilantism threatens the country's domestic reform, internal tranquility, and ability to conduct meaningful diplomacy. If these groups are operating with money and equipment provided by the most senior Iranian officials, then the Iranian government cannot shirk its responsibility for their actions. Expanding trade and offering too many diplomatic or economic "carrots" to the government will not remove the threat posed by the vigilantes. Rather, nonviolent reform can triumph in Iran only if hardliners recognize that their actions will not be tolerated by the Iranian government or by the outside world.

Notes

1. For an example of the venom in Iran's official historiography directed toward the United States in this regard, see "Amrika va Jang-i Tahmili" (America and the imposed war), in *Rahbiteh-i Siah* (*The black relation*) (Tehran: The Political Office of the Agency Representing the Basij Resistance Forces of the Vali-yi Faqih, 1994), pp. 137–210.

2. Guy Dinmore (*Financial Times* correspondent), interview by author, Washington, DC, July 19, 2000.

3. "General Pardon for Those Who Have Fled," *Iran*, December 8, 1999, in FBIS-NES-2000-0103.

4. Hasan Yusifi Ishkaviri, "On Margin of Khurdad Tribunal: Common Literature," *'Asr-i Azadagan*, October 31, 1999, p. 2.

5. Murtaza Nawruzi, "Raising Forqans," *Bayan*, May 11, 2000, p. 6.

6. *Iran Statistical Yearbook 1376 [March 1997–March 1998]* (Tehran: Statistical Center of Iran, Islamic Republic of Iran Planning and Budget Organization, 1998), p. 706; author conversation with U.S. State Department official, December 1999.

7. Wayne Mapp, *The Iran–United States Claims Tribunal: The First Ten Years, 1981–1991* (Manchester, United Kingdom: Manchester University Press, 1993), p. 4.

8. State Department Noon Briefing, October 5, 1999, transcript provided by Federal News Service.

9. Ambassador Michael Sheehan, "The Battle against Terrorism: Report from the Administration" (lecture delivered at The Washington Institute for Near East Policy, October 12, 1999).